MOUNT OF ACES

THE ROYAL AIRCRAFT FACTORY S.E.5a

PAUL R. HARE

FONTHILL

Austin-built B8275 served briefly with 29 Squadron but crashed on 31 May 1918 and was written off.

Fonthill Media Limited
Fonthill Media LLC
www.fonthillmedia.com
office@fonthillmedia.com

British Library Cataloguing in Publication Data:
A catalogue record for this book is available from the British Library

ISBN 978-1-78155-288-9

Typeset in 9.5pt on 13pt Sabon LT
Printed and bound by CPI Group (UK) Ltd, Croydon, CR0 4YY

Connect with us
 facebook.com/fonthillmedia   twitter.com/fonthillmedia

CONTENTS

Edward 'Mick' Mannock seated in his S.E.5a at London Colney before his squadron's departure to France.

James McCudden seated in an S.E.5a. He considered it to be 'a most efficient fighting machine'.

INTRODUCTION

Were you to ask an ordinary man in the street to name a British fighter plane of the First World War, he would probably, after some deliberation, say the Sopwith Camel. This oddly named aeroplane has become well known, possibly because it was flown by 'Biggles', the fictional hero whose exploits were avidly read by schoolboys for generations. However, in reality, Britain's top scoring aces preferred to fly the Royal Aircraft Factory's S.E.5a. Edward 'Mick' Mannock (sixty-one confirmed victories) 'revelled in its superior performance', while James T. B. McCudden (fifty-seven victories) 'liked it immensely' after his first flight in it, and later called it 'a most efficient fighting machine', scoring fifty-one of his victories flying an S.E.5a, twice bringing down four enemy aircraft in a single day.

The South African Andrew Beauchamp-Proctor scored all of his fifty-four victories in S.E.5as. Cecil Lewis, who flew it with 56 and 61 Squadrons, described it in his autobiography as 'the last word in fighting Scouts'. W. Sholto-Douglas, later Marshal of the Royal Air Force Lord Douglas of Kirtleside, who commanded an S.E.5a Squadron in 1917-18, considered it to be 'one of the most beautiful aeroplanes ever built', and declared it to have been 'the most successful of the many single-seat fighters that we employed in the war', arguing that among its many attributes, it retained much of its performance at high altitudes, which the Camel did not. It was at least as fast as all of the opposing German fighters in level flight, and faster than any in a dive. It was also more manoeuvrable than its enemy. Albert Ball, Britain's top-scoring fighter pilot at the time of the S.E.5's introduction, did not like it at first, but later came to appreciate its rugged strength, scoring nine victories flying it.

The former test pilot Harald Penrose (1903-96), who flew an S.E.5a towards the end of the 1920s, said of it in the second volume of his classic history of British aviation prior to the outbreak of the Second World War:

> I flew an S.E.5 and found it very similar to a Moth, though lateral control became much heavier with speed, until in a dive of 140 mph, brute force was necessary,

Albert Ball, England's top fighter pilot at the time the S.E.5 was introduced, didn't initially take to his new mount but later came to appreciate its rugged strength.

The pilots of 85 Squadron in front of their aircraft.

giving the impression of sluggish response, although in fact proportional to the amount of aileron applied ... In other respects it was delightful; firm in normal behaviour owing to the general stability, which made it a good gun platform, and directionally kept true in a dive with little change of rudder trim between slow speed and high.

Even the adverse yaw produced by the downward moving aileron was a mild virtue, as it required noticeable rudder to counteract it, and still more to make the turn, so it was easier for a heavy-footed pilot than the Camel's tendency to swing instantly into a turn if directional trim pressure was momentarily released.

A modern day pilot who has flown a preserved S.E.5a in flying displays confirms that its very good longitudinal stability would have made it fairly easy for even an inexperienced pilot to track his intended target and to keep it in his gun sights.

As well as being fast, manoeuvrable, and a superb gun platform, it was easy and very pleasant to fly. Perhaps the finest endorsement of its qualities as a flying machine is the fact that amateur builders have over the years produced more reproduction S.E.5s than almost all of the other types of First World War fighters put together.

Original examples remained in use with civilian operators well into the 1930s and during the 1950s. A restored example was put back in the air, and has remained so – serviceability permitting – ever since, so that in all but one of the ten decades that have passed since its first flight there has been at least one S.E.5, real or reproduction, active in our skies; a truly remarkable achievement by an equally remarkable aeroplane.

F871, built by Wolseley Motors, with 94 Squadron at Le Hameau. The wheel discs have been painted with the squadron's markings.

1

ANCESTRY

The S.E.5 was, not unnaturally, the fifth in the S.E. series, although its ancestry was not quite as straight forward as that statement suggests, for the Royal Aircraft Factory's system of designations was occasionally, and sometimes deliberately, both arbitrary and obscure. The first of the series was the S.E.1, a Canard (tail first) biplane, its designation standing for 'Santos Experimental No. 1', Santos-Dumont having been the first man to fly in Europe, and his machine, the 14-Bis, having been a Canard. At the time of the S.E.1's construction in spring of 1911, the Farnborough establishment, then known as H. M. Balloon Factory (it became the Royal Aircraft Factory in April 1912 upon the creation of the Royal Flying Corps), lacked authority to build new aeroplanes. The S.E.1 was its first design since 1908 when aeroplane experiments were suspended, and H. M. Balloon Factory claimed the new machine was a 'reconstruction' of a crashed Bleriot XII monoplane sent to the factory for repair. Only the engine, a 60-hp ENV type 'F' was reused, and the tractor monoplane emerged from the workshops as a pusher biplane with a forward elevator and twin rudders mounted just to the rear of the propeller, but too far apart to be within its slipstream. The fuselage was covered, and the skid-mounted wheels were positioned aft of the centre of gravity, with a skid under the nose. The wings had rounded tips and were rigged in two bays, with ailerons on the top wing only.

Research had indicated that the Canard layout would provide the greatest possible safety and control, a conclusion reached independently by the Wright brothers when they started their own experiments some ten years previously. However, the first flight, made by its designer Geoffrey de Havilland on 8 June, highlighted some instability in pitch, which successive modifications lessened, but failed to wholly eliminate. The only real improvement occurred at the end of the month when the all-moving forward elevator was replaced with a fixed surface, having a hinged elevator at its trailing edge.

Then on 18 August, the S.E.1 was taken up against advice by Theodore J. Ridge, the factory's assistant superintendent, who lacked de Havilland's experience as a pilot.

A Bleriot XII similar to the one from which the S.E.1 was ostensibly reconstructed. (*Via Leo Opdycke*)

The S.E.1 as originally built, surrounded by workmen and the inevitable schoolboys who seemed to turn up wherever an aeroplane appeared.

A rear view of the S.E.1 showing the chain drive to the propeller. The dark patches on the fuselage sides are radiators for the water-cooled ENV engine.

Unable to manage the tricky machine, Ridge spun while attempting a turn, crashing to the ground and sustaining injuries from which he died later that same day. The machine, which had failed to live up to expectations, was not rebuilt, and the 'Santos Experimental' series was discontinued. It thus had no direct link to the S.E.5.

The first of the S.E.5's true forebears began life as the B.S.1, or Bleriot Scout No. 1, a designation intended to classify it as a fast, single-seat tractor design. The restriction on the building of new designs had in part been lifted and replaced by a requirement that prior approval be obtained from the War Office before any such project was put in hand. However, the 'reconstruction' ploy would continue to be used on occasion to circumvent this requirement. Therefore in January 1912, Mervyn O'Gorman, the factory's superintendent, submitted for approval a short list entitled 'Suggested Aeroplanes for Construction', containing various types that he thought would aid the factory's aeronautical research, which included a high-speed aeroplane capable of at least 90 mph, but landing at no more than 60. This was the B.S.1.

Approval was granted and the machine was built to a design by Geoffrey de Havilland, who was then the factory's chief designer as well as its test pilot. The machine was powered by a 100-hp Gnome rotary engine, but with provision to fit an even more powerful engine should one become available. It was the world's first high-speed Scout, pre-dating by several months the Sopwith Tabloid for which such a distinction is frequently claimed. Its fuselage was of a circular cross section to reduce drag, with the forward part, to which the wings and undercarriage were attached, being built around four longerons faired round with formers and stringers, with the rear portion, aft of the cockpit, being a true monocoque. The

The B.S.1/S.E.2 on Farnborough Common outside the Royal Aircraft Factory. The joint between the two halves of the fuselage is clearly visible aft of the cockpit.

wings were of RAF6 aerofoil section, the most efficient then available, with neatly rounded tips, and were rigged with single-bay bracing. Lateral control was by warp. A fuel tank, divided longitudinally to house 21 gallons of petrol and 11 gallons of oil, was mounted in the top decking between the engine and the cockpit, with the instruments fixed to a board mounted directly to the back of it. These comprised a tachometer, column air speed indicator, altimeter, compass, and a watch. The completed machine had an empty weight of just 850 lb.

By now, the Royal Aircraft Factory had revised its system of aircraft nomenclature, replacing the category 'Bleriot Scout' with 'Scouting Experimental', and so it was as 'S.E.2' that the machine made its first flight on 13 March 1913, piloted by de Havilland. Although it flew well and responded well to its controls, its performance being all that was expected of it, directional control was poor, due to the rudder clearly being too small. De Havilland therefore had a larger rudder put in hand, but continued to test it with the original rudder, recording a top speed of 92 mph and a climb of 800 feet per minute.

On 27 March, de Havilland was flying S.E.2 over Farnborough Common and initiated a turn while at about 100 feet. However, the machine entered a spin, which he was unable to correct with the inadequate rudder. He thus crashed, suffering two sprained ankles, a broken jaw, and the loss of some teeth.

In submitting an accident report to the War Office, O'Gorman suggested that the machine be rebuilt with an 80-hp engine to slow it down, estimating the cost of the repair at £900, plus a further £425 for the new engine. Approval was given, after due consideration to the fairly large sums involved, on 25 April.

Work on the revised design was carried out by Henry Folland, with some input from E. T. Busk, whose speciality was aerodynamic stability. The machine was rebuilt with a similar wing structure to the original, but with a wholly new fuselage and tail surface. The new 80-hp Gnome engine was enclosed in a neat cowling, and the rear fuselage tapered more sharply than previously, and was fitted with both dorsal and ventral fins. The bottom edge of the high aspect ratio rudder was shod in steel for use as a tailskid, and there was a spring rudder post to absorb shocks. A new, semi-circular tailplane and elevators with a slight inverse taper further replaced the original design. The undercarriage was also modified, the rear skids being more upright than previously, bringing the wheels further forward, with radius rods provided to retain the axle. The empty weight was now just 740 lb, the reduction being largely due to the smaller engine.

The first flight of the rebuilt S.E.2 took place on 12 October, and appears to have led to some doubt over the adequacy of the fin area, although this may have been a legacy from the previous version, as no further adverse comments were made and the fins were never altered.

Although the rebuilt S.E.2 could no longer be considered as a high-speed machine, O'Gorman hoped to retain it at the factory for experimental purposes while building another machine as a high-speed Scout, this time with a 160-hp

The S.E.2 rebuilt, showing the conventional construction of the rear fuselage.

engine. However, on 23 December 1913, he was instructed by the War Office that S.E.2 was to be handed over to the RFC for service use.

O'Gorman protested that the machine was not only an experimental design, but that it had a number of faults that still needed to be rectified, including a broken skid and cracked cowlings. Yet the War Office was adamant, and with only the skid repaired, it was handed over on 17 January 1914 and assigned to 5 Squadron with the serial 609. By late March, its condition had deteriorated further and it was returned to the Royal Aircraft Factory for overhaul. It emerged from the workshops with the monocoque replaced by a new rear fuselage of conventional construction, a smaller tailplane, new vertical tail surfaces, and a separate skid. The undercarriage had been replaced with another of similar design, and the streamlining improved by the addition of a small spinner to the propeller boss, as well as the replacement of the main bracing cables by streamlined section swaged 'Rafwires'. It was now designated the 'S.E.2 Rebuilt' and returned to service on 20 October, serving with 3 Squadron in France as a fast Scout. It returned to the depot in March 1915, being unfit for further service.

Although not allowed to retain the S.E.2, O'Gorman did get his chance to build a machine with a 160-hp engine and a fourteen-cylinder, two-row Gnome 'Lambda Lambda', then probably the most powerful rotary aero engine commercially available. The instruction to proceed was given in December 1913.

Preliminary work that had begun on the S.E.3, which was to have been a single-seat Scout with a 100-hp engine, was therefore abandoned in favour of the 160-hp S.E.4. However, some innovative features of the design, such as single interplane struts and full-span ailerons that could be used together as flaps and reflexed upwards to reduce drag at high speeds, were incorporated into the more powerful machine.

Henry Folland, who had become head of the design department on the departure of Geoffrey de Havilland, undertook the design work. He incorporated every available method of reducing both weight and drag, and accepted a factor of safety slightly lower than the usual figure of three in some components where an increase in strength would result in additional drag. His intention was quite simply to create the fastest aeroplane in the world.

The wings were identical to those of S.E.2 in both area and plan form. They were rigged with only a very shallow dihedral and without stagger. The wings were of RAF6 section, set at an angle of incidence in level flight of just over 2 degrees, and covered with a Ramie fabric that was lighter than the usual linen. The single interplane struts were of 'I' shape. Their ends flared to attach to both wing spars, and the bracing wires were streamlined section 'Rafwires'. Fixing bolts were recessed to finish flush with the surface, and the cables to the ailerons were routed within the hollow centre section struts. As in the S.E.3 project, the ailerons could be lowered together to act as landing flaps and reflexed to reduce the wing camber, and thus both lift and drag at high speed, although the speed variation gained in either function was less than 5 mph. The gaps between moveable and fixed surfaces were covered with a fine elastic net, which it was hoped would further reduce drag.

The fuselage was built around four longerons, and in two halves, as was common practice, so that the forward section that carried the engine wings and undercarriage could be of a more substantial cross section than the rear. The top and bottom were covered with plywood for rigidity and the sides were cross-braced with wire. The whole was faired round with formers and stringers after wind tunnel tests indicated that the resulting reduction in drag would compensate for the increase in weight. The whole fuselage was plywood covered, and the engine enclosed in a neat cowling with a large conical spinner fitted to the four-bladed propeller, leaving only a narrow, annular gap to admit air to the engine. A hole was formed in the nose of the spinner to admit more air and aid cooling, although this may not have been included in the original design.

The tail surfaces were similar to those of the S.E.2 and included both dorsal and ventral fins, as favoured by Folland, and appeared almost symmetrical about the fuselage centre line. The tailplane was set at a slightly lower angle than that of the wings, but could be adjusted on the ground up to 3 degrees either way. The undercarriage comprised an inverted tripod of three struts, with a transverse leaf spring that carried the wheels mounted on its apex. Yet perhaps the most innovative feature of all was a moulded celluloid canopy, which fully enclosed the cockpit. However, no pilot could be persuaded to fly the machine with this fitted, claiming with some justification that it distorted the view.

The completed machine had an empty weight of 1,082 lb, and to keep the loaded weight down to 1,350 lb, the tank had fuel for flight of just 1 hour.

It was competed by 17 June 1914, and following inspection, Norman Spratt, who had taken over as the factory test pilot after de Havilland was transferred to the Aeronautical Inspection Department, began flight trials. However, the surface of Farnborough Common proved too much for the undercarriage; the machine rolled so badly when taxiing that the wing tips touched the ground and no take off was possible. The machine therefore had to be returned to the workshops, where it was fitted with a conventional wooden vee undercarriage, with the axle bound to the apexes by rubber shock cord. At the same time, the spinner was modified, with fan blades fitted to its inner surface in order to increase airflow, and a small conical spinner was attached to the propeller boss to reduce turbulence with the outer spinner.

The first flight was made with Norman Spratt in the uncovered cockpit on 27 July, and the top speed was recorded at 134.5 mph, making it, as intended, the fastest aeroplane in the world. Climb was equally impressive at 1,600 feet per minute, although its landing speed of 52 mph was considered too fast for service use and it was not therefore recommended for production. However, at the outbreak of war on 4 August, every available aeroplane was sorely needed, and it

S.E.4 on Farnborough Common with its original tripod undercarriage, which although highly innovative, proved impractical, rolling excessively on the rough ground of Farnborough's airfield.

was adopted by the RFC, given the serial 628, and painted with a primitive and rather unnecessary camouflage scheme.

It would appear that, before being handed over to the RFC, the S.E.4's engine was changed to a 100-hp Gnome and a two-blade propeller was fitted, presumably to reduce its performance, especially its landing speed, to something more manageable. On 12 August, Norman Spratt took it up for a test flight. As he came in to land, the starboard wheel collapsed and the machine somersaulted onto its back, wrecking it completely, fortunately without any serious injury to Spratt. It had served its purpose and was not rebuilt.

The S.E.4a, on which work began soon after the demise of the S.E.4, was not, as its designation would suggest, a development of the earlier machine, but a wholly separate design, although its appellation may have been chosen to infer a connection with what had after all been the world's fastest aeroplane. Henry Folland was again in charge of the design, but appears to have left most of the detailed work to his assistants. It was intended that as well as being fast and manoeuvrable, as its scouting designation would suggest, the S.E.4a should also be stable and easy to manage. Thus, as well as the full-span ailerons, the wings

The final form of S.E.4, with a vee undercarriage and with camouflage and the serial number 628 applied.

included a generous 3.5 degrees of dihedral. The mechanism to use the ailerons together as landing flaps, as in the S.E.4, was included in the design. There was no separate centre section; the two wings joined at the centre line and were supported on struts that formed an inverted 'v' when viewed from the front, with their apexes at the joint between the wings. The lower wings were attached to tubular stub spars projecting from the fuselage side, and the wings were braced in a single bay with a pair of parallel interplane struts each side, securely cross braced, and with an additional flying wire at mid-gap. The fuselage was built around a conventional box girder of four longerons, and as usual, was constructed in two halves joined at the rear of the cockpit. The forward portion was of welded steel tube and the rear portion of spruce, with its top and bottom surfaces covered in plywood for rigidity and the side cross braced with wire. Unlike previous S.E. designs, the fuselage remained flat-sided, although as a gesture towards streamlining, a head fairing was built into the top decking. The tailplane and elevators were straight, with raked tips and the vertical surfaces similar to those of the S.E.4. The undercarriage was the now usual vee of steel tube, faired to a streamline shape with wood, and the tailskid was mounted directly to the stern post, its spring enclosed in a fairing that acted as a continuation of the lower fin. The 80-hp Gnome engine was enclosed

The first S.E.4a, 5609, with a mounting for a Lewis gun above the upper wing.
Reloading would have been virtually impossible in flight.

in a neat cowling, manufactured in two pieces, and drove a two-blade propeller.
Semi-conical fairings neatly blended the round cowling into the flat sides of the
fuselage.

Although at one time it did appear that volume production was contemplated,
in the end just four examples were built, all by the Royal Aircraft Factory, the first
of which, serial 5609, was submitted for inspection on 23 June 1915. It made
its first flight, piloted by Frank Goodden, the factory's new chief test pilot, two
days later. This machine differed from the original design, and from the other
three examples, in having a number of aerodynamic refinements; the fuselage was
faired to a circular cross section with formers and stringers, the stub struts to
which the lower wings were attached were faired to an aerofoil section, a conical
spinner was fitted to the propeller, and the cable runs to the lower ailerons were
run internally within the wings. Unfortunately, the effect of these refinements has
not been discovered. A mounting for a Lewis gun was fitted above the upper wing
so that it could fire clear of the propeller, although it was so far out of the pilot's
reach that reloading would have been impossible.

The second example, 5610, was built as originally designed, with the control
cables exposed to facilitate maintenance, the fuselage flat-sided, and the lower
wing roots uncovered to allow the pilot a downward view. It was completed ready
for its final inspection by 16 July, and made its first flight five days later, achieving
a top speed of 90 mph. It was taken over by the RFC, and stationed for a time on
home defence duties at Joyce Green, near Erith in Kent, for which it was fitted

S.E.4a 5611 in flight.

with a Lewis gun mounted on the upper wing, although there is no evidence that the gun was ever fired in anger.

The third example, 5611, was initially fitted with an 80-hp Le Rhone engine, and was retained at the Royal Aircraft Factory for testing. It was later fitted with an 80-hp Gnome, and then in 1916, with a Clerget of similar power. Extensive testing of the multi-function ailerons demonstrated that wound down together for use as flaps, they could reduce the landing speed from 45 mph to 40 mph, and when reflexed at speed, improve performance by just 2 mph. In neither case did the advantage justify the complication of operating them, and they appear never to have been so used in normal operations. 5611 was still flying at Farnborough in September 1917, but in common with the two previous S.E.4as, its eventual fate is unknown.

The last S.E.4a built, 5612, was completed in September 1915, and after fairly brief testing, served with the RFC on home defence duties, stationed at Hounslow. On 24 September, it was flown several times by Capt. Bindon Blood, a distant relation to the Thomas Blood who attempted to steal the Crown Jewels in 1671. While practising steep turns, Blood lost control and spun to the ground. The petrol tank split in the crash and the machine was immediately enveloped in flames, with Blood suffering severe burns from which he died the following day. The inquest returned a verdict of accidental death.

2

BIRTH OF THE S.E.5

In February 1916, Brig.-Gen. Hugh Trenchard, commander of the RFC in France, set out his requirements for the aeroplanes needed to carry the war on into 1918, which included a fighting aeroplane with the following minimum performance criteria:

Climb to 10,000 feet within 15 minutes.
Have a speed of at least 100 mph at 10,000 feet.
Reach a ceiling of at least 18,000 feet.
Have an endurance of 4 hours (although 3 hours could be accepted).
Preferably be a two-seater, but may be a single-seater.
Have the ability to fire straight in front.
Performance to be achieved with a full load, including 500 rounds of ammunition.

When the War Office passed on these requirements to the aircraft industry, several manufacturers responded, including the Royal Aircraft Factory, whose proposal of course became the S.E.5. Just as the S.E.4 had been built to take advantage of the potential offered by a specific engine, so too had the S.E.5, in this case the compact Hispano-Suiza V8.

Soon after the outbreak of the war, the Hispano-Suiza company had switched its efforts from luxury motor cars to aero-engines, and by February 1915, an example of their products, a 11.76-litre V8, was submitted to the French Ministry of War's standard test at the company's works at Bois-Colombes. This test required it to be run at full power for 10 hours, which it did successfully, producing 140 hp. The engine, designed by the company's co-founder Marc Birkigt, was a quantum leap forward in engine design; instead of the separate cylinders of contemporary types, each of its banks of four cylinders was cast from aluminium in one piece, with all gas and water passages formed internally, and with screwed-in steel cylinder liners threaded along the whole of their length to ensure the best possible heat transfer.

The remarkable Hispano-Suiza V8 engine. This example is preserved in a museum in New England.

Cylinder heads were also of cast aluminium, and included an overhead camshaft, fully enclosed valve gear driven by vertical shafts and bevel gears at the rear of each cylinder block. The cast aluminium components were coated in vitreous enamel to ensure that there were no leaks. The pistons were also aluminium, with a pair of tubular connecting rods sharing each crankshaft journal in a blade and fork arrangement, with the blade having a bearing that covered the whole crankshaft journal, and the fork running on the outside of that. The four-throw crankshaft was arranged in a single plane and supported in five bearings, the middle three being plain with a ball race at each end. The crankcase was split along the centre line of the crankshaft, and the deep, almost conical sump added to the engine's stiffness. A positive oil pressure was maintained to the main bearings and valve gear, the surplus simply draining by gravity back to the sump. Two 8-cylinder magnetos were fitted, driven by the vertical shafts through small bevel gears, with two spark plugs fitted to each cylinder. The carburettor was mounted between the cylinder block, the aluminium inlet manifolds being partially enclosed in the water jackets. Empty and without a radiator, the engine weighed just 445 lb. Its fuel

Sectioned 150-hp direct-drive Hispano-Suiza HS8Aa in a museum in Madrid.

consumption was just 0.5 lb per hp-hour (i.e. about 10 gallons per hour) and oil consumption just 6 pints per hour.

Rival engine manufacturers were aghast at this new competitor, and appear to have persuaded the Ministry that the engine should not be adopted until it had been tested for 50 hours; an arbitrary figure they appear to have thought no engine could ever achieve.

This was done, commencing on 21 July 1915 at the French Government aeronautical research establishment at Chalais Meudon, on the outskirts of Paris. Again the engine passed with ease and was immediately adopted for production as the HS-8Aa, with a power output of 150 hp.

It may have been this test that the RFC's senior staff officer Col. H. R. M. Brooke-Popham witnessed; he was so impressed that he immediately recommended that an order be placed. The initial order for fifty completed engines was placed in August. In addition, a licence to manufacture it in England was sought, although this took some time to negotiate and was not agreed until the end of February 1916, as the company was based in Barcelona, the French manufacturer being merely a subsidiary. The Wolseley Motor Co. of Birmingham, who already manufactured a water-cooled V8 of their own, as well as building other V8s under licence, were selected to produce the engine in England, with further orders being placed in France until they could gear up for production.

The first example received by the RFC around February 1916 was fitted by the depot at St Omer to a B.E.2c, an obsolescent, two-seat reconnaissance machine that was then the most numerous type in service. The new engine almost doubled the power of the B.E.2, and made it faster, although no less obsolescent. Good sense prevailed, with future engines being reserved for more deserving designs.

Early in 1916, Brig.-Gen. W. S. Brancker, then assistant director of Military Aeronautics, and therefore in charge of RFC supplies, appears to have visited the Royal Aircraft Factory at Farnborough to suggest that they should design a fighter aeroplane around the new engine, something they would have been almost certain to do even without this official encouragement. Mervyn O'Gorman, the factory's superintendent, initially discussed the project with Frederick M. Green, the factory's chief engineer, and William Farren, who had replaced the late E. T. Busk as head of the aerodynamics department.

The need to fire directly ahead was the most serious consideration. The remainder of Trenchard's requirements were more easily met given the new engine, for although several synchroniser gears, which would allow a machine gun to fire forwards without hitting the propeller, had recently been designed, they remained rather crude and unreliable. Initially, two entirely separate proposals were considered.

The first proposal, developed by senior design engineer John Kenworthy, was an attempt, as previously tried in both the French SPAD A2 and in the Royal Aircraft Factory's own B.E.9, to combine the aerodynamic advantages of a tractor design with the clear field of fire afforded by a pusher. This was to be acheived by housing the pilot in a nacelle mounted ahead of the propeller and supported from an extension of its shaft. Designated 'Fighting Experimental No. 10', or F.E.10, it was a neat, well-considered if slightly dated design, with the fuel tank immediately below the engine to concentrate the heaviest items together and improve manoeuvrability. The centre section struts were splayed outwards to clear the engine mounted beneath them, making the centre section wide, and the wings were of unequal span, the upper overhanging the lower by 5 feet each side. Extensive testing had shown this arrangement to improve aerodynamic efficiency. The fuselage tapered sharply aft of the engine, its small cross-section reducing both weight and drag. The pilot's position gave him a superb forward view, and the proposed armament, a pillar-mounted Lewis gun, gave him the best possible forward field of fire. However, the surviving preliminary general arrangement drawings dated 25 July and 1 August 1916 show the gun rather close to the pilot's face, a problem that would no doubt have been resolved had the concept been developed further, but it was abandoned in favour of a more simple tractor design, work on which had begun at about the same time.

Credit for the original concept sketch from which the S.E.5 was developed has always been given to the test pilot Frank Goodden, but all the detailed work was carried out by Henry Folland who filled an entire notebook (Army book type 134) with stress and load calculations. By 21 May 1916, Folland had calculated

The S.E.5's fuselage frame showing details of the construction, including the extensive cross bracing that kept the whole thing rigid.

The first page of Henry Folland's notebook, containing his design calculations for the S.E.5, with the estimated weights of the various component parts. (*Via RAE Museum*)

Detail of the engine bearers showing the plywood bulkheads, which gave the rigidity essential to support the mass of the engine.

the loaded weight of the design at 1,696 lb, including 500 lb for the engine and radiator, 120 lb for armament, 180 lb for the pilot, and 310 lb for fuel, oil, and water, leaving just 586 lb for the fully covered and rigged airframe. He was assisted by William Farren and H. Grinstead, who carried out further stress calculations.

Preliminary drawings produced at this time show a neat little biplane, fairly conventional in layout, with equal span and single-bay wings; its design intended to keep manufacture as simple as possible.

Initially, the wings were to have been set at an angle of incidence of 4 degrees, and given 3.5 degrees of dihedral, but a wind tunnel test on a model of the proposed design showed some instability, and therefore both angles were increased to 5 degrees, thus solving the problem. At the same time, the wings were moved forwards 5 inches from the original position in order to adjust the position of the centre of gravity. A general arrangement drawing, A16058, dated 15 June 1916, is titled 'Scheme 1', and shows a plan view with the wings in their original position, with a note added that they are to be moved forward, while a side view, A16057, produced by a different draughtsman and dated the previous day, shows them in the correct, amended location. Other differences between the two schemes included a slightly lower thrust line for Scheme 2; the engine was mounted lower so that it could be more fully cowled. Curiously, both schemes show a geared

Close-up of cockpit area showing the supports for the seat, the tubular members which joined to the wing spars, and the two spring loaded doors for the steps.

engine, which had yet to be completed, with a Lewis gun mounted in the cockpit and firing via a long blast tube though the propeller boss, eliminating the need for any synchroniser gear.

The preparation of construction drawings began around the end of June. With the desire to keep manufacture simple, while at the same time ensuring the best possible performance, the final design had straight lines and simple curves wherever possible, with meticulous attention to every detail.

The fuselage frame was the now usual box girder, built in one piece, of four spruce longerons, with struts and cross member also of spruce, cross braced with slender threaded steel rods screwed directly into the metal fittings, those at the sides always having the right hand thread to the bottom. All fittings throughout the machine were formed from mild steel; Folland's extensive calculations had shown that no higher grade of steel was required. The rearmost bay of the fuselage, which tapered almost to a point, making cross bracing less effective, was covered with ply for additional stiffness. The engine bearers were of ash, strengthened by transverse bulkheads formed of spruce and covered in plywood for stiffness. The engine was fully enclosed, except for its cylinder heads, which projected at each side and to which small fairings were fitted to aid streamlining. A car-type frontal radiator was fitted, its top curved to match the contour of the engine cowling. A hole in its centre made way for the propeller shaft, the hole being oval in shape to accommodate the differing sizes and positions of the direct drive and geared engines. The two-blade propeller was 9 feet in diameter. The main fuel tank held 28 gallons and was immediately behind the engine; its top was shaped to match the cowling and the forward fuselage. A simple, semi-conical celluloid windscreen offered protection to the pilot's face, and a small window helped illuminate the

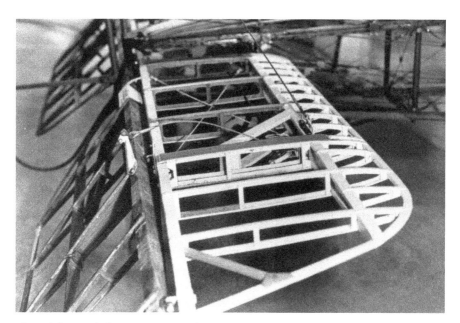

The tailplane and elevators uncovered.

instruments, which comprised an altimeter, air speed indicator, RAF pattern compass, rev. counter, fuel and oil pressure gauges, and a watch. A radiator temperature gauge was fitted, although no way of adjusting engine cooling was provided. A simple switch controlled the ignition, and a hand-operated magneto was fitted to assist in engine starting. The fuel gauge was mounted directly to the rear of the tank, simplifying its installation, if not its use. A rotary selector switch allowed petrol to be fed to the carburettor from either the main or service (gravity) tanks, or to be transferred between tanks. The tailplane incidence could be adjusted by means of a wheel at the side of the cockpit driving an endless chain, and the pilot was secured to his seat with a broad lap strap. A holder for a Very pistol and a rack of cartridges completed his equipment. The rear decking was of a regular cross-section, tapering to the rear, and comprised of plywood formers and light spruce stringers. A hinged spring-loaded footstep door was fitted on each side of the fuselage to aid entry into the cockpit. The floorboards forward of the pilot's seat were fitted directly to the underside of the lower longerons and the seat position could be adjusted, fore and aft, to accommodate pilots of differing heights. The fabric to the fuselage side was laced on, the joint running along the upper longeron to allow access for maintenance.

The centre section struts were steel tube, with the aileron control cables run inside, faired to a streamline shape with spruce fairings bound with cloth tape. These struts were splayed outwards, as the upper centre section, with a span of 4 feet, was wider than the fuselage. The lower wings were attached to stub spars

Detail of the underside of the wing structure showing the relative delicacy of the main ribs and the additional riblets, which maintained the shape of the leading edge.

An uncovered aileron showing the construction.

formed of steel tubing projecting from the fuselage side. It was originally planned that these stubs would be enclosed in fairing, which would extend little further than the span between them to give the pilot a downward view, but this was later changed to a fully aerofoil shaped fairing; triangular cut outs were provided in the lower wing roots to provide the downward view. The pilot was seated high so that his eye line was close to the trailing edge of the upper wing, limiting its intrusion into his field of view to the narrowest possible arc. An angle of just 9 degrees is shown on the side view drawing, although the actual angle would of course be dependant upon the pilot's height. The wings were of RAF15 aerofoil section, rigged in a single bay, but with an additional flying wire from the fuselage to the compression ribs at mid bay. Naturally, bracing was with streamlined 'Rafwires'. Ailerons were fitted to all four wings, the tips of which were sharply raked outwards to a shape that wind tunnel tests had indicated reduced the loss of lift due to turbulence in the airflow over the wing. The spars and ribs were of spruce, the rib spacing varying slightly according to the calculated load carried, with additional false ribs forward of the main spar to maintain the leading edge profile. Drag and anti-drag bracing was by means of threaded tie rods. Header tanks for petrol and oil were to be built into the leading edge of the upper wing, their pipes running through the hollow centre section struts, along with the control cables. The tailplane and elevators were also spruce; their shape was similar to those fitted to the S.E.4a, and pivoted about its front spar to alter the tailplane's incidence, controlled by the wheel in the cockpit. The original drawings had indicted a rudder area of 6 square feet, and a fin area of 3 square feet, but when in August 1916 calculations indicted that a greater fin area would be needed, John Kenworthy, who was supervising production of the drawings, simply substituted the vertical surfaces from his own F.E.10 design for those previously drawn by Folland. These were formed around frames of steel tubing, with spruce ribs to maintain shape.

The fully sprung tailskid, which had originally been shown attached directly to the rudder, was fixed to the stern post instead in a neat fairing that continued the lower fin, with the rudder being cut away to accommodate it. The main undercarriage legs were of steel tubing, faired to a streamline section, with diagonal cross bracing to the forward set only. The one-piece axle was enclosed in a streamlined fairing, with teardrop fairings over the rudder shock cord that attached it to the vees of the undercarriage legs. The wheels were standard 500 x 100 wire wheels, fabric covered to reduce resistance.

Design work was completed around the end of August, with every component fully detailed ready for manufacture, as was standard Royal Aircraft Factory practice.

3

PROTOTYPES

Three prototypes were ordered in September 1916 on a direct War Office instruction to the Royal Aircraft Factory, where Henry Fowler had now replaced Mervyn O' Gorman as superintendent. No procurement contract was required for this instruction, the factory being under direct War Office control, although it appears that one, No. 87/A/392, was issued anyway, presumably in error. On the same day as this contract was issued, 28 September 1916, the serial numbers A4561-4563 were allotted to the three machines.

Around the end of September, the factory finally received its first two Hispano-Suiza engines from the order placed over a year previously. These were H5213/WD10100, which was fitted to A4561, and H5193/WD10104, which went into A4562.

A4561 was completed almost exactly as designed, but was unarmed as the planned Lewis gun installation was not possible with the direct-drive engine. The exhaust manifolds were long enough only to cover the four exhaust ports on each cylinder bank, their discharge directed sideways from the middle of the manifold by a short outlet. A 9-foot diameter, two-blade propeller, No. 14588 (type T28041), was fitted, completing A4561, which was submitted for inspection at midday on 20 November. Approval for flight was given the same evening.

The next day, it was prepared for its first flight; the tanks were filled, the oil checked, and the radiator topped up. After lunch, it was wheeled out onto the airfield where a number of senior members of staff had gathered to watch. Frank Goodden climbed into the cockpit, the propeller was swung, and the engine coughed, but failed to start. It was swung again and then again, with no sign of life from the Hispano-Suiza. After several people had tried swinging the propeller, the spark plugs were removed, heated, and replaced, but still the engine showed no signs of life; with dusk fast approaching, it was wheeled back to the sheds.

The following morning, A4561 was again brought out. This time, the engine started easily; a small auxiliary petrol tap near to the instrument panel in the pipe from the gravity tank to the carburettor had been discovered and turned on.

The first prototype S.E.5, A4561, with Frank Goodden in the cockpit, probably before its first flight on 22 November 1916.

A4561 after modification with overwing gravity tank, extended windscreen and modified exhausts. A Vickers gun has been fitted, but not a Lewis.

Goodden took off at about 10.00 a.m.; on landing after a 20-minute flight, he is said to have exclaimed, 'She's a pixie,' although a more formal appraisal of the new machine's flying qualities was also made.

Goodden flew A4561 again the next day, 22 November, this time for 25 minutes. At 12.25 p.m., it was taken up by Capt. Albert Ball, then Britain's leading 'ace', who was in England on leave. Ball flew the S.E.5 for 10 minutes, but returned to

Another view of A4561 after initial modification, showing the plain radiator.

earth less enthusiastic than Goodden had been, for he thought it less agile than the little Nieuport he currently flew in France. He was, in any event, pinning his hopes on the AFB1, then being developed by Austin Motors, the design for which he had had some input.

The second prototype, A4562, was completed about a week after the first, and differed from it in having a propeller-driven air pump mounted beneath the cockpit, whereas the A4561's was engine driven. It was approved for flight on Friday 1 December, with Goodden taking it up for its first flight on the following Monday. Two days later, it was flown by Lt Roderic Hill, then with 60 Squadron, who in February 1917 joined the Royal Aircraft Factory staff as test pilot. A4562's performance was measured, and it was recorded as having a top speed of 127.5 mph at 1,000 feet, and 116 mph at 9,000 feet. Climb to 5,000 feet was accomplished in 4 minutes and 55 seconds, and it reached twice that height in a total of 12 minutes and 25 seconds. Loaded weight was 1,827 lb, more than Folland's original estimate, but such increases were almost inevitable as a design developed.

A4562 appears to have suffered an accident at about this time, although the circumstances and the pilot's name have not been discovered. None the less, it was taken into the workshops for both modification and repair, and did not re-emerge for several weeks.

10 December saw A4561 flown to Hounslow, where it was to remain until 2 January 1917 for evaluation by service pilots. On 17 December, Capt. William Sanday of 42 Reserve Squadron, based at Hounslow, reported that the semi-

conical windscreen would not allow the pilot sufficient access to a Vickers gun, were one to be fitted, to clear jams. There appears to be no record of which other pilots, if any, flew it while at Hounslow, for it was Sanday who flew it back to Farnborough on completion of the evaluation.

Sanday's comment about the Vickers gun was far from idle speculation, for on 21 December, A4562 emerged from the workshops with just such a weapon installed. The Vickers gun was offset slightly to port of the aircraft's centre line, and a depression was formed in the top of the petrol tank to accommodate it. It was operated by the newly developed 'CC' synchronising gear, designed by the Rumanian engineer George Constantinesco. This gear operated hydraulically, and unlike mechanical gears, could be fitted to any combination of gun and engine. The Vickers gun was fitted with both a simple ring and bead sight, and an Aldis optical sight, to give pilots a choice according to personal preference. A hatch was formed in the starboard side of the forward decking, through which the ammunition belt was loaded, with a long access panel on the port side for servicing the gun. The muzzle of the gun was supported by two steel struts mounted on the top longerons, with the rear supported on a bracket fixed to the instrument panel, and a chute for spent cartridge cases was taken out through the floor. Possibly at the suggestion of Albert Ball, who favoured such a weapon, being accustomed to using it on his current mount, the Nieuport, a Lewis gun on a Foster mounting was fitted to the upper centre section, firing clear of the propeller arc. Both guns were angled upwards at 5 degrees, their lines of fire set to converge at 150 yards. Separate triggers, mounted on the control column, were provided for each gun, allowing them to be used independently if necessary. The windscreen sides were extended to afford the pilot some protection if he had to deal with a jammed gun. The header tank was eliminated from within the upper port wing and replaced with a tank fitted externally above the wing root, possibly to simplify production. Repairs, following A4562's probable accident, had included the provision of a new undercarriage and rear skid, the replacement of the bottom rib to the top fin (part 2/10364), and the propeller (T.28051/14591). Some fuselage cross bracing was duplicated at the same time. The seat was now adjustable to three positions to accommodate pilots of differing heights, and was fitted with what was described as '0.5-inch mock armour'. The centre section had also been replaced, the new one having a slightly enlarged cut-out in the trailing edge, and the exhaust manifolds had been modified, or replaced, with the outlets now at the rear; the middle position had been found to create turbulent gas flow. These modifications completed, Frank Goodden flew A4562 for 15 minutes on 22 December, and then two days later, he flew it to the depot at St Omer for further evaluation. On Boxing Day, it was flown by Lt Frederick Selous of 19 Squadron, which was then being re-equipped with the SPAD VII, also powered by the 150-hp Hispano-Suiza engine, for a comparison between the two types. Selous noted:

I flew the S.E.5 at St Omer and noticed the following points:

> Control Elevator: The S.E.5 is slightly lighter in the elevator than the SPAD,
> but the machine is harder to keep in a steep dive.
> Laterally: There is not any difference between the S.E.5 and the SPAD.
> View: The view in all directions is very good, and much better than the SPAD,
> especially forwards and downwards.
> Climb and Speed: This cannot be judged accurately without flying the
> machines together, but the S.E.5 has a much greater range of speed than
> the SPAD and will fly at 45 mph.
> General Flying: Although the S.E.5 is stable, it can be manoeuvred quite as
> well as the SPAD. The S.E.5 can be landed slower than the SPAD and has a
> much flatter glide.

Lt Roderic Hill, then a Nieuport pilot with 60 Squadron, also test flew A4562 on
the same day as Selous, and demonstrating his ability as a future test pilot, prepared
a report comprising three foolscap pages of close typing, praising almost every
aspect of the S.E.5 in comparison with the Nieuport and SPAD. He concluded:

> The S.E.5 has, in my opinion, certain advantages over the Nieuport and SPAD:
> Its speed is good; it involves little strain on the pilot; it lands as slowly as the
> Nieuport and more slowly than the SPAD; it is stronger than the SPAD; its gun
> mounting is superior. Its disadvantage with respect to the Nieuport is that it
> cannot be manoeuvred with quite the same rapidity, although at high altitudes,
> manoeuvres should be possible with a much smaller loss of height.

The following day, 27 December, Brig.-Gen. J. F. A. Higgins, commander of the
RFC's Third Brigade, who was present during these test flights, also reported his
opinion of the new machine, stating:

> I have inspected the S.E.5 and saw it flown by Maj. Goodden and Lt Selous (No.
> 19). Lt Hill (No. 60) also flew it. The pilots' report that it is quick fore and aft,
> but not as quick as either the SPAD or Nieuport. They report that the view is
> very good. I consider that this is correct. It appears to give 127 or 128 mph on
> the indicator at 500 feet. The speed range is astonishing, I should put it at 45 to
> 125 mph. It appears easy to fly and strong. In my opinion, it is the best single
> seater I have seen. The instruments and fittings seem to be suitably placed.

Although opinions were clearly very favourable, a number of relatively minor
modifications were requested, including: the provision of a knob on the tailplane
trim wheel; the fitting of the gun triggers on sliding sleeves so that their position
could be adjusted for individual pilots; the provision of an engine decelerator

Changing drums on the Lewis gun was simple enough on the ground, but much more difficult when flying; pilots often found it necessary to break off combat, or descend to a lower altitude to do it. The gun could also be fired in this position to attack an enemy from below. The photograph features a machine from 1 Squadron RFC and was taken at Clairmarais aerodrome on 3 July 1918.

mounted on the control column; the removal of the ring and bead sight; the fitting of an extended loading handle to the Vickers gun; the repositioning of the release lever for the Lewis gun from the spade grip to the pistol grip and the removal of the spade grip; the provision of a rack for the storage of spare Lewis gun ammunition drums; the fitting of inspection doors over the pulleys in the control cables within the wings and tailplane; and the addition of some means of varying the amount of radiator surface exposed to the airflow.

On 31 December 1916, Brig.-Gen. Robert Brooke-Popham, then quartermaster general, ordered the depot to carry out these modifications and to have them completed by 6.00 a.m. on 2 January 1917. This was a tall order, but the staff at the depot did what they could, leaving the major modifications to be carried out on the machine's return to the factory. As part of these modifications, a locker was provided on the starboard side immediately aft of the cockpit by forming a shelf on the top longeron and fitting a hinged door in the decking. This was originally intended to house a wireless, but although none was ever fitted, the locker remained and was incorporated in the revised drawings prepared as a result of the modifications, and so appeared in all production machines.

Lt Selous flew A4562 back to Farnborough on 4 January, arriving at 4.30 p.m., whereupon it was taken into the workshops for the remainder of the requested modifications to be carried out. As part of these, the Vickers gun was fitted with an extended loading handle, which was easier for the pilot to operate; the Hyland Type 'E' eventually became standard for the type. The rack for two ammunition drums was fitted on the left of the instrument panel – the instruments being rearranged to make room – with another rack at the pilot's right side, just aft of the rudder bar. The work was clearly far more involved than Brooke-Popham had realised, as A4562's next flight, following completion of the requested modifications, was not until 26 January. Thus modified, A4562 set the standard for production machines. A4561 was modified to the same standard, although there is no evidence that it was ever fitted with a Lewis gun.

Meanwhile, the third prototype, A4563, was completed and fitted with a 200-hp engine, No. H7019/WD10111, which had left the factory in France on 28 November 1916. The additional power was largely achieved by an increase in rotational speed to 2,000 rpm, a speed then thought too fast for a direct-drive propeller, necessitating the addition of a reduction gear, as envisaged in the S.E.5's original design. This modification reduced the propeller speed to an efficient level, and incidentally, also reversed its direction of rotation. The gear ratio was 41:24 giving a propeller speed of 1,170 rpm, and since the reduction gear also raised the thrust line, a larger diameter propeller could be used to take advantage of the additional power while maintaining the same clearance between its tips and the ground.

The second prototype, A4562, after being fitted with its guns. Although not visible in the picture, it had also been fitted with a gravity tank on the upper port wing root. It appears to be being prepared for flight.

The third prototype, A4563, with a 200-hp engine, seen at Martlesham Heath in May 1917. This was after extensive modification to bring it to production standard, although the headrest fairing is of an unusual shape.

A4563 after modification. The higher thrust line of the geared engine is apparent.

Another view of A4563 after modification.

A4563 was fitted with the centre section and the upper port wing removed from A4561; the leading edge of the wing shows a fabric patch where the tank had been removed. It was unarmed, and apart from the engine, a radiator of a slightly different design, and an external gravity tank, it was identical to the originally built A4561.

It was submitted for final inspection at 11.00 a.m. on 12 January 1917, the approval note being issued just 85 minutes later. At 1.15 p.m., Frank Goodden took it up for the first time, staying aloft for 15 minutes. On 18 January, he took it up for a climbing test lasting 40 minutes, demonstrating that although only slightly faster than the 150-hp version, it climbed significantly quicker. It would also prove to have a much higher ceiling. The next day, Goodden flew it again for 20 minutes in what was logged as an 'engine test', and then for just 10 minutes on 24 January to test a Claudel carburettor, which had replaced the original Zenith. The effect of the substitution has not been recorded. It was not to fly again until 30 April.

4

A TRAGEDY

At 11.00 a.m. on Sunday 28 January 1917, a clear, frosty morning, Frank Goodden took off in A4562 to continue testing it after modification. Some 8 minutes later he was flying back towards the factory from the direction of Cove at a height of around 1,500 feet when the port wing cell suddenly collapsed. Goodden was seen to throw out his helmet and goggles and appeared to be trying to stand up in the cockpit, perhaps intending to jump clear as the falling aeroplane neared the ground. However, he was still in the cockpit when A4562 hit the ground and received injuries from which he died instantly. An inquest held at Cambridge Military Hospital in Aldershot returned a verdict of accidental death.

An investigation was held into the cause of the crash, eye witnesses agreeing that the struts had came come out as the wings folded up. It was therefore concluded that either the drive wheel for the CC gear, which could not be found among the wreckage, had flown off and had struck the struts, knocking them out, or that the propeller had broken and a piece had struck the strut. A. P. Thurston, the respected aeronautical engineer employed by the War Office at the time, was dissatisfied with both theories. At first he collected all the fragments of the propeller from the crash site, recovering well over 90 per cent of its total weight, sufficient to prove that it had still been intact at the time of the crash. He next drew out the wing structure in chalk on a convenient floor, and laid out the recovered components on it in order to established where and how the collapse had occurred. He concluded that it had failed in downward torsion, as would occur during certain manoeuvres such as pulling out from a dive, or beginning a loop, as it was believed that Goodden had been doing at the time of the wing's failure. On examining the wings of A4561, which had by then flown about 35 hours, he noted that the internal bracing was slack, and also saw signs of incipient failure in the spar, from which he deduced that the compression ribs, although perfectly adequate to perform their function of resisting the fore and aft forces upon the structure, could flex up and down, and so both put strain on the spars and allowed the struts to come loose. He recommended that a plywood web should be added to these ribs between the spars to provide sufficient stiffness to prevent the flexing.

Above: A group of staff officers examine the second prototype, A4562, which had the mid-position exhaust outlets and a propeller-driven air pump beneath the fuselage. Frank Goodden is seated in the cockpit.

Left: Frank Goodden, the Royal Aircraft Factory's chief test pilot, was killed testing the S.E.5.

With the thoroughness that typified the Royal Aircraft Factory, A4561, its engine removed for re-use, was then tested to destruction, proving Thurston's conclusion to have been correct. The report BA86 was published in April 1917.

Henry Folland, who had been responsible for the design of the wing structure, felt responsible for Goodden's death and resigned from his position at the Royal Aircraft Factory. He was, however, later persuaded to return to aircraft design and joined the Nieuport & General Aircraft Company as its chief designer.

An investigation was made into the strength of the S.E.5 by Royal Aircraft Factory engineers and scientists. The results were published, as was usual for the Royal Aircraft Factory, in an Advisory Committee for Aeronautics' Report & Memorandum (No. 491) in April 1917 for the benefit of the whole aircraft industry. Its summary read:

> The wings will bear 5.5 times normal loading, but will then fail under shear at a point in the front spar just inside the wing strut connection. A strengthening of the upper wing spars at this point would increase the strength of the wing as a whole. The upper wing spars are also weak for failure in a longitudinal plane under compression. The fuselage is much stronger, relatively, than the wings.

The solution to increasing the shear strength of the spars was simply to thicken them slightly, reducing the amount of routing. The aerodynamics department, under William Farren, also discovered that the overhang outboard of the struts was weaker than intended. Rather than redesigning the entire wing to incorporate a new rear spar, it was decided simply to reduce the length of the overhang by shortening the spar to achieve the required strength, thus reducing the rake of the wing tips and decreasing the span from 28 feet to 26 feet and 7 inches.

The drawings for the new, reduced span wings bear the designation S.E.5a, this being, at least in the eyes of the Royal Aircraft Factory, the true distinction between the two types. However, the rigging notes, produced later for the instruction of mechanics in the field, were titled 'S.E.5 – 150-hp Hispano-Suiza' and 'S.E.5a – 200-hp Hispano-Suiza', and these rigging notes had a far wider distribution than the manufacturing drawings, leading to the erroneous belief that it was engine size, rather than wingspan, that distinguished an S.E.5a. In service, both variants were usually called S.E.5s, or simply just S.E.s, blurring the distinction between them.

5

PRODUCTION BEGINS

Such was the obvious potential of the S.E.5 design that an order was placed with the Royal Aircraft Factory for a production batch of twenty-four aircraft fairly soon after the order was made for the three prototypes, again on direct War Office authority, rendering a purchase contract unnecessary. The serial numbers A4845-4868 were allotted on 5 October 1916. These had the original 28 feet span wings, although following Goodden's fatal crash, the compression ribs were modified during construction, as were the strut/spar joints, causing some slight delay to their completion.

The first of the batch, A4845, was generally as the modified A4562, including the propeller-driven air pump, but with a much larger windscreen intended to afford the pilot even better protection when dealing with problems with the Vickers gun; the forward decking was cut away within the area covered by the canopy to facilitate access. The Aldis sight was positioned high above the fuselage, close to the top of the windscreen, to meet the pilot's eye line. A4845 was fitted with a 150-hp direct-drive Hispano-Suiza engine, No. 10054/WD10119, built under licence by Societe Anonyme des Automobiles Aries of Villeneuve-la-Garenne, to the north of Paris, which drove propeller No. 16797 (T28051), a slight modification from that of the prototypes. The exhausts were also modified, and now had their outlets at the front of the manifold. It was submitted for its final inspection at 8.40 a.m. on Thursday 1 March, but approval was not given until 7.50 p.m. the following day, suggesting that it was subjected to a very thorough examination, as might be expected following the fatal crash of A4562.

Its test flying programme was carried out under the supervision of Roderic Hill, who had previously flown A4562, and who in February 1917 had joined the Royal Aircraft Factory as head of the Experimental Flight, replacing the late Frank Goodden. Later in March, following the completion of testing, it was flown to the RFC's Aeroplane Experimental Station, which had recently moved from Upavon to Martlesham Heath in Suffolk, for evaluation.

Its rate of climb, perhaps because of the change of propeller type, was found to

The first production S.E.5, A4845, which was completed by 1 March 1917. The greatly enlarged windscreen and the high position of the Aldis sight are noteworthy.

be slower than with tests of A4562 the previous December, but in the evaluation report No. M84 other aspects of the machine were more heavily criticised, especially the effectiveness of the ailerons, despite the S.E.5 having been judged to be as manoeuvrable as the SPAD. The report stated:

> Lateral control insufficient, especially poor at low speeds, hence the machine manoeuvred poorly and was almost uncontrollable below 70 mph in gusts, causing a crash in getting off on 29/3/17. Suggest that aileron control be geared higher.
> Windscreen unnecessarily large, hindered the pilot's landing view.
> Time for complete turn of 360 degrees: 12 seconds.
> Length of run to unstuck: 95 yards; to pull up, engine stopped: 105 yards.

The crash mentioned in the report cannot have been serious, as the machine was soon back in the air. Overall, the test pilots at Martlesham Heath were more complementary than the above report suggests, recognising the S.E.5 as a significant improvement over previous types. The suggested modification to the

A8904, showing the reduced rake of the wing tips that distinguished the S.E.5a. It was completed on 26 April 1917. Like the entire second production batch, it had shutters over the upper part of the radiator.

aileron gearing was made by simply altering the length of the control horns, which were tested by three pilots of the factory's Experimental Flight, Capt. Roderic Hill, Lt D. V. Armstrong, and Lt John Noakes. They all agreed that lateral control was now much better than in the original design, although all thought that the ailerons were still not as effective as they might have been. The modification was therefore incorporated into production standards as soon as possible.

Aileron design, like many aspects of aerodynamics, was then still in its infancy, with bigger always being considered better. The adverse yaw caused by the additional drag created by the down-going aileron meant that, like all aeroplanes of this period, a lot of rudder was needed to make a controlled turn.

All twenty-four machines in this production batch were completed and inspected by 30 March, although engine deliveries had obviously been a problem, as twenty-one of them, including A4845, had Aries-built engines, with A4851 receiving engine No. 5690/10108. A4861 had an engine built by the French Hispano-Suiza company; A4862 was fitted with the engine removed from the prototype A4561, which had been tested to destruction; and A4868 got the first engine No. 627/2233/WD8202, built under licence by Wolseley Motors. Their propellers were

This machine is believed to be A8916, which after completion by the Royal Aircraft Factory, was tested a Martlesham Heath and at the Central Flying School. The small spinner fitted to the propeller boss is an unusual, and rather pointless feature.

equally dissimilar, with seventeen of the batch having type T28051, six having type T28066, and A4864 having a T28041, as fitted to the first two prototypes.

A4850, which was completed on 7 March 1917 and fitted with engine No. 10046/WD10115 and propeller No.16801, type T28051, passed final inspection on 14 March, and was the first to be handed over to the RFC. Following final inspection, the remainder were all taken over by the RFC, most seeing active service, although one, A4849, with its engine removed, ended up at the School of Technical Training, near Reading, as an instructional airframe.

A second batch of machines, A8898-8947, was ordered, again on a direct instruction from the War Office, at the end of December 1916; deliveries began towards the end of April 1917. These differed from the first batch in having shutters fitted to the upper portion of the radiator, controlled by the pilot, and shorter span wings with reduced rake to their tips, which made the Royal Aircraft Factory regard them as S.E.5as. They were still fitted with the large windscreen, the high seating position, the forward outlet exhaust manifolds, and initially, the exposed gravity tank on the upper centre section.

Some were fitted with French-built, 150-hp engines, and others with engines

A8910, a typical machine from the second production batch, showing the forward outlet exhausts and the large 'greenhouse' windscreen.

Another view of A8910 showing the Lewis gun on its foster mounting.

The instrument panel was mostly dedicated to management of the engine and its fuel systems, with flight instruments limited to a compass, air speed indicator, and altimeter.

built by Wolseley Motors. Those with Wolseley engines included the first example A8898 (668/2233/WD8240), which was approved on 20 April, A8903 (667/2233/WD8244), which was approved 23 April, A8904 (668/2233/WD8240), A8911 (657/2233/WD8232), and A8922 (699/2233/WD8274), which was approved on 25 May. A number of the batch, including A8906, A8921-27, A8927, A8935, A8938, and A8941-47, were fitted with the 200-hp engine, their apparently random selecting being dictated by the availability of engines. A8923 had the first 200-hp engine built by Wolseley (Adder No. 782/2233/WD8357), and was inspected on 30 May 1917, making its first flight the same day. All of these different engine required different propellers, French-built engines having different bosses to those made in England, and geared engines needing coarser pitch propellers than those with direct drive, which rotated faster.

Deliveries were completed by the end of June 1917, with three examples, A8938, A8943, and the last of the batch, A8947, being retained by the factory for experimental purposes.

6

INTO SERVICE

56 Squadron RFC had begun forming up in June 1916, its initial cadre of personnel being transferred from 28 Squadron, and by the end of February, it was stationed at London Colney under the command of Major R. G. Bloomfield.

On 15 March, Albert Ball, who had joined the squadron as a flight commander, went to Farnborough to collect its first S.E.5, A4850, which had passed its final inspection the previous day. His arrival at London Colney was rather disappointing to those waiting on the ground for a sight of the new machine with which they were to be equipped; he landed quietly without performing any of the expected aerobatics. His prejudice against the type, formed during his brief test flight nearly four months previously, was clearly undiminished by further experience. A4853 was received by the squadron two days later, and further machines, including A4847, A4862, and A4863, arrived during the remainder of the month, until by early April, the squadron was fully equipped. The S.E.5 was thus in squadron service before the Martlesham Heath report was prepared, but the pilots of 56 Squadron needed no outside help to condemn the overly large windscreen, quickly naming it the 'greenhouse', and claiming that it not only distorted vision, but that its sharp edges would be dangerous in a crash.

The modification was first made to A4850, which Major Bloomfield had assigned to Ball as his personal mount; the cut out in the forward decking was filled in and the 'greenhouse' replaced with a small, Avro-pattern screen of triplex safety glass. Two bracing wires were fitted to locate the rear of the Foster mount, which had previously been fixed to the frame of the windscreen, and the Aldis sight was lowered to suit the new pilot's eyeline. However, Ball did not stop there; the adjustable seat support was replaced with one of plain wood, on which the standard padded wicker seat was mounted, enabling the pilot to sit lower in the fuselage, and the centre section was replaced with one having an internal gravity tank and a slightly larger trailing edge cut out. A small head fairing was fitted, and for some reason, the standard 700 x 100-mm wheels were replaced with 700 x 75-mm wheels from a Bristol Scout.

Albert Ball, seated in A4850 at London Colney on 6 April 1917. The replacement centre section, with its enlarged trailing edge cut out, is obvious, as is the Avro windscreen and the head fairing. The gravity tank was now internal and the seat had been lowered by 8 inches. The rear of the Foster mounting was held in place with bracing wires, all other examples having a metal bracket.

A4853, the second S.E.5 to join 56 Squadron, arrived on 15 March and is seen here as it was originally built. It was modified before going to France to have an Avro windscreen and a lowered seat.

The modifications to the windscreen and seat were also made to A4853 while the squadron was at London Colney. Minor problems with the Vickers guns and their CC synchronising gears were left alone until the squadron got to France; reliance was placed upon the Lewis guns, with which the majority of the pilots were already familiar.

Ball had the Vickers gun and CC gear of A4850 removed altogether, allegedly to save weight, and the petrol tank replaced with one without the indentation into which the gun fitted, thereby gaining a small increase in fuel capacity. He then had a Lewis gun fitted to fire downwards through the cockpit floor, although for what purpose he never made clear, as aiming the weapon would have been a matter of luck.

But still Ball wasn't satisfied, expressing all of his disappointment and prejudice in a letter home:

> The S.E.5 has turned out a complete dud, its speed is only about half Nieuport speed [it was actually slightly faster – author] and it is not so fast in getting up. It is a great shame, for everybody thinks they are so good, and expects such a lot from them. Well, I am making the best of a bad job. If Austin will not buck up and finish a machine for me, I shall have to go out on an S.E.5 and do my best. I am getting one ready. I am taking the gun off in order to save weight. Also I am lowering the windscreen to take off resistance. A great many things I am taking

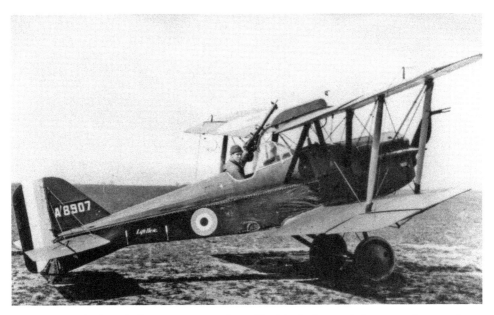

A8907 as built with short span wings, but still with the large windscreen and external gravity tank. Albert Ball is in the cockpit. The machine was delivered to 56 Squadron on 7 May 1917, the day Ball had his fatal crash.

Thirteen S.E.5s of 56 Squadron lined up at London Colney, ready for the squadron's departure to France on the morning of 7 April 1917.

off in the hopes that I will get a little better control and speed. But it is a rotten machine and if Austin's machine is not finished I am afraid things will not go very OK.

The squadron suffered a loss before it even went overseas; on 3 April, Lt J. Leask, flying A4857, got caught in a blizzard, lost control, and came down in the sea.

Just before noon on 7 April 1917, the squadron left London Colney for France. Thirteen S.E.5s, led by Lt Cecil Lewis, landed at the depot at St Omer for lunch, and then flew on to Vert Gallant, an airfield near the road from Amiens to Doullen, which they were to share with two other squadrons. The reliability of the Hispano-Suiza engine allowed 56 Squadron to become the first to fly out to France without losing any machines due to engine failure en route. However, the next day they rather blotted their copybook when Lt Arthur Rhys-Davids turned A4847 over upon landing after a practice flight. Rhys-Davids was unhurt, but the machine was extensively damaged and eventually written off.

2/Lt W. B. Melville stands by his S.E.5, A4852, at London Colney, prior to 56 Squadron's departure for France.

Immediately upon arrival, the Squadron was visited by Brig.-Gen. Brooke-Popham, who with typical efficiency, accepted that the S.E.5 should be modified. The next day, he issued the following order to the 9th wing, of which 56 Squadron now formed a part:

1. The following alterations will be made to the S.E.5s of No. 56 Squadron:
   a) The present windscreens will be taken away and a simple three-ply cowling with an Avro windscreen at the rear will be substituted, similar to the sample machine I was shown yesterday.
   b) The present adjustable and armoured seat will be taken out and a simple board fitted across. This should be placed somewhat lower than the lowest position of the present seat.
   c) The gun mounting for the Lewis gun must be made to fit better and the slide lengthened by about 2 inches so that cover from the Avro windscreen is afforded when changing drums. No. 2 Aircraft Depot will assist the squadron in making extensions for the slides.
2. The squadron commander will be given a free hand as regards details of the above alterations provided that all twelve machines of the squadron are the same.
   Please note that the Vickers gun is to be left where it is. The design of two Lewis guns that is in Capt. Ball's machine is not approved, but this machine need not be altered back again.
3. Instructions regarding the removal of the gravity tank on the top plane will be given as soon as certain information has been obtained from England.

9 April, which was Easter Monday, saw the opening of the Battle of Arras and the Canadian assault on Vimy Ridge. 56 Squadron was not in action, as arrangements were being made for the modification of their machines. Ball flew A4850 the short distance to No. 2 depot at Candas for further modification to be made a pattern upon which modifications to the unaltered machines could be based as quickly as the depot were able. Other modifications included the provision of radiator shutters, as being introduced on production machines, and the replacement of the small propeller-driven air pump under the fuselage by one driven directly by the engine, as in the first prototype A4561. At least one machine was fitted with long exhaust pipes, modified from those of a SPAD, to prevent fumes from entering the cockpit. This modification also became standard for all machines; Major Mead conveyed details of all the changes made in France back to England on 17 April.

Two days after having stated that Ball's machine need not be altered, Brooke-Popham evidently changed his mind, and gave instructions that the downward firing Lewis gun was to be removed and a Vickers gun refitted. No replacement petrol tank with the depression to accommodate the gun was available, the original having been left in England, and so the gun was fitted in a fully exposed position on top of the tank.

On 14 April, Brooke-Popham gave an instruction that the over-wing gravity tanks were to be removed from four of 56 Squadron's aircraft, and that these were to be temporarily flown without. On the same day, Maj.-Gen. Hugh Trenchard,

A8917 has the large windscreen, but the gravity tank is now internal.

commander of the RFC in France, wrote to the technical director general at the War Office asking that fourteen new centre sections, complete with in-built gravity tanks for petrol and water, should be sent to France as soon as possible. He also made enquires into the potential effects of shortening the wingspan and the consequent reduction in the area of the ailerons, pointing out, 'The squadron reports that lateral control at low speeds is by no means good.'

This latter issue was, as we have seen, already in hand, but on the matter of the tanks, the Royal Aircraft Factory responded that twelve centre sections, complete with tanks, were being made and would be sent overseas as soon as possible, adding that the production drawings had already been similarly amended.

In an effort to get 56 Squadron into action as soon as possible, No.1 Depot at St Omer was also instructed to make six sets of tanks for fitting by the squadron's own ground crews. It was sent a centre section, probably that from A4847, which had been deemed beyond repair, to ensure a good fit. The modifications were all complete by 19 April, and the pilots of 56 Squadron spent the next two days making numerous practice flights to assess how the changes might have affected the performance and handling of their machines.

Finally on 22 April, they flew their first patrol with five aircraft, led by Ball, taking off at 10.18 a.m., although with strict orders not to cross the lines. They spotted an enemy reconnaissance machine and Ball closed in to attack, but failed to bring it down. A similar patrol by 'B' flight, later in the day, saw no enemy aircraft at all. The next day, 56 Squadron made its first patrols over the lines; 'C' flight took off at 6.00 a.m., but returned without having seen anything. However, at 10.45 a.m., Ball took off alone in A4850 and encountered an Albatros two-seater near Adinfer, but as he began his attack, his Lewis gun jammed after just five rounds and he landed at Le Hameau to rectify the problem. Taking off again at 11.45 a.m., he spotted a group of five enemy Scouts and attacked them, firing about 150 rounds from his Vickers gun before one fell in flames. The remainder turned on Ball, putting bullets through his fuselage and wings, and he dived away, the S.E.5 easily escaping from his pursuers. Later in the same patrol, he attacked another two-seater; using his favourite tactic of flying underneath and pulling down the Lewis gun to fire upwards, he fired about half a drum into it, wounding the observer and forcing it to land. On examination, it was discovered that several of the bullets that had hit Ball's machine had pieced the wing spar. Due to the strength of the S.E.5's construction, he had not even been aware of it.

Although Ball was the only pilot to score that day, squadron morale was high, and higher still when the next day brought three more victories, shared among the pilots involved. The pilots were now pleased with their S.E.5s, especially its ability to break off combat and dive away at will. However, combat had revealed the need for a further modification, as the centre section was unable to cope with the recoil of the Lewis gun mounted on it, this never having been included in the original design.

On 25 April, Brooke-Popham wrote a further instruction to No. 2 Depot at Candas regarding 56 Squadron's S.E.5s, stating:

> It has been found that the present centre sections are not sufficiently strong enough to stand the blast of the overhead gun. You will therefore send these centre sections to your aeroplane repair section immediately they arrive for the following alterations to be made:
>
> a) The central former rib to be removed and a strong rib substituted. The flange (web) of this rib is to be quarter inch ash, with ash flanges of corresponding strength; these ash flanges to be cut down in thickness where they pass over the main spars so that the height of the gun mounting remains the same.
>
> b) Three-ply to be put on as covering over the top of the centre section between the front and rear spars. Fabric to be placed over the three-ply and continued back to the trailing edge.

These modifications were quickly made without the squadron ceasing operations, the only remaining problem with the S.E.5 being repeated gun jams caused either by faulty ammunition or by problems with the CC gear, although this did not stop the combat victories mounting up, with Albert Ball very much the squadron's star turn.

On 27 April, Ball suffered damage as a result of anti-aircraft fire, but managed to return home with his wings damaged, bracing wires shot away, and only his port-side elevator operational; he knew that again he owed his life to the sound construction of the S.E.5. A4850 was transported later the same day to the depot at Candas for repair. The next day, pilot Lt Gerald Maxwell was also hit by anti-aircraft fire, and he too had occasion to be grateful for the rugged construction of his S.E.5 A4863, for the shell fragments hit his forward fuselage, stopping the engine and damaging his elevator controls. The machine came down near Combles, the engine breaking out as it struck the ground and the remainder of the wreck bouncing along for about 100 yards. Maxwell was still strapped in, but when it came to rest he was completely unhurt.

30 April saw the squadron suffer its first combat casualty when Lt Maurice Kay, in A4866, was shot down and killed during a combat with some Albatros Scouts.

Replacement aircraft were now being received from the second production batch, with the shortened wings. A8898, for example, was with the squadron by 1 May when it was flown by Albert Ball. Lt J. H. Flynn overturned A4855 while landing on 4 May, the machine being sent to No. 2 Depot at Candas for repair, returning to the squadron in June fitted with a 200-hp geared engine. The next day, Lt H. Meintjes suffered engine failure and overturned A4848 on landing; a common problem that would later be improved by a modification to the undercarriage to move the wheels forward.

Above left: The cockpit area with the large 'greenhouse' windscreen and external tank. There is no ammunition drum fitted to the Lewis gun and only one in the rack in the cockpit. The Aldis sight is not fitted.

Above right: The cockpit area after the design was modified. This machine has its Foster mount raised on a streamlined block to clear the higher thrust line of the geared 200-hp engine. The Aldis sight is missing, although its mounting brackets are in place ahead of the windscreen.

Ball continued to fly A4858 while waiting for A4850 to be returned from the depot. On 2 May, he led Lt Knight and Lt Lehman on a patrol, during which several enemy aeroplanes were spotted, although their attacks were frustrated by continual gun jams. However, in the evening, Ball took off alone and added an Albatros two-seater to his score. The next day, in a letter to his fiancée Flora Young, Ball wrote, 'The general is giving me two S.E.5s, so I shall be OK,' confirming that he had finally put his faith in the design, although he was still experiencing problems with gun jams, with more occurring the next day.

At 5.30 p.m. on 7 May, a patrol of eleven S.E.5s took off from Vert Gallant led by Ball in A4850, which had now been returned from the depot. The others were: Lts Maxwell (A8902) and Knaggs (A8904) from 'A' flight; Capt. Crowe (A4860), Lt Chaworth-Musters (A4867), Lt Rhys-Davids (A4868), and Lt Leach (A4856) from 'B' flight; and Capt. Meintjes (A8900), Lt Hoidge (A4862), Lt Lewis (A4853), and Lt Melville (A4861) from 'C' flight. Three hours later, after several

C5303 of 56 Squadron has an unusual extended pistol grip fitted to the Lewis gun, probably because its usual pilot was not very tall.

combats with groups of enemy fighters from Jasta 11, just five had returned. Two pilots, Capt. C. M. Crowe and Lt Rhys-Davids, later reported having landed at other airfields. Two more, Lt Meintjes (A8900) and Lt J. O. Leach (A4856), were in hospital with wounds. However, Lt R. M. Chaworth-Musters,who had broken away from the group to carry out a solo attack, and Albert Ball, who in just seventeen days had brought down nine enemy aircraft flying the S.E.5, were dead. Ball was not shot down in combat, but it appears that after diving away, he came out of cloud too low to flatten out and struck the ground. His death was recorded as a flying accident, but was still keenly felt.

As was RFC policy, replacement pilots and aircraft quickly arrived and 56 Squadron carried on, patrolling and scoring victories in their S.E.5s. On 31 May, the squadron moved north to the airfield at Entrée Blanche, ready for the battle of Messines, which would start on 7 June.

7

MASS PRODUCTION

Meanwhile at the Royal Aircraft Factory, the third prototype, A4563, which had been grounded following Goodden's fatal accident, was modified to become, in effect, the prototype for production S.E.5as, although its headrest fairing was of a non-standard shape and its radiator shutters were full height. It had the strengthened, shorter span wings, and its 200-hp Hispano-Suiza engine drove a four-blade propeller, type T8096, which would become standard for engines with the 24:41 reduction gear. On completion of testing at Farnborough, it went to Martlesham Heath, being flown there by Roderic Hill on 29 May. The report on its performance, No. M105A, stated that it had a top speed of 121 mph at 15,000 feet, an altitude it could reach in 18 minutes and 50 seconds, and that its ceiling was 22,000 feet. Lateral control was considered 'better than the S.E.5', and the small windscreen improved the view, especially for landing. The report did note, however, that the control cable runs and the Vickers gun were not easily accessible for maintenance. Once testing was complete, it was handed over to the RFC, joining 56 Squadron on 11 June, when Cecil Lewis collected it from the depot.

The first production order, other than those previously given to the Royal Aircraft Factory, was placed with Martinsyde Ltd who were awarded contract No. 87/A/1616 on 1 February 1917, well before A4563 was modified or had flown. The order was for 200 aircraft, and deliveries were to take place as soon as possible at a rate of between three to six machines each week. On 6 April, contract No. 87/A/1627, also for 200 aircraft, was placed with Vickers Ltd for their Weybridge works. In view of the larger size of the long-established armaments contractors, they were expected to deliver between six to ten machines a week.

An order for 100 S.E.5as was placed with the Whitehead Aircraft Company of Richmond in Surrey on 22 February, but was later cancelled without any aircraft being delivered.

Further orders were placed with the Royal Aircraft Factory, Austin Motors Ltd, Bleriot & SPAD Ltd of Addlestone in Surrey, which later became The Air Navigation, and with Wolseley Motors Ltd, who were also building versions of

S.E.5as under production at Vickers' Works, Weybridge. (*Brooklands Museum*)

the Hispano-Suiza engine, the 150-hp direct-drive Wolseley Python and the geared 200-hp Adder.

These machines were all to be S.E.5as to the revised design produced by the Royal Aircraft Factory, and were to be fitted with the 200-hp Hispano-Suiza engine, built by various contractors. Deliveries of Wolseley Motors' version of the engine, the Adder, began in March 1917; licence-built examples from Peugeot appeared in April, from Basier in June, and from DFP, Delauney-Belleville, and Emile Mayen in August. The higher thrust line of the geared engine moved the tips of the propeller into the path of bullets from the Lewis gun, and so the Foster mount was raised on two streamlined spacer blocks to regain the necessary clearance.

Changes arising as a result of modifications in service were introduced into production machines as they occurred. This practice was made inevitable by placing orders before development was complete, but one that would eventually lead to confusion and dissatisfaction among manufacturers.

The first contractor-built machine, B501, from Vickers, was delivered to Martlesham Heath for evaluation on 5 July 1917. It had by that time already passed inspection and acceptance tests, although the date for its initial receipt by the RFC is not known. However, the second machine, B502, had been delivered by the end of June and sent to France, where on 13 July, it was issued to 56 Squadron.

C6414, from the first batch built by Wolseley Motors, under construction in March 1918. The carefully posed photograph shows near clinical conditions. (*Peter H.T. Green collection*)

C9051 outside the works of Austin Motors around June 1918, showing an immaculate finish. The gentleman in the trilby hat occupying the cockpit has not been identified.

B607, from the first batch built by Vickers' Works, Weybridge. It served at the Wireless Experimental Establishment at Biggin Hill, Kent, where the elevated location aided reception range.

Deliveries quickly reached the rate required by the contract, with three machines, B505, 505, and 506, all being delivered on 6 July. B507 followed the next day, and the last of the batch, B700, was completed by mid-November, by which time a new contract had been placed. Manufacture thereafter was continuous.

Martinsyde's first example, B1, was with the RFC early in July, but the second appears to have been delayed by several weeks, and only seven had been accepted by the end of August. Deliveries finally reached the contract rate of between three and six each week in September, the batch being completed with the delivery of B200 on 20 February 1918, by which time, as with Vickers, a new contract was in place.

Delivery of the Royal Aircraft Factory's batch of fifty machines began with B4851, which was shipped to France on 2 August. One example, B4856, went to the Officers' Technical School of Instruction at Henley-on-Thames, and was received there in September; the last of the batch, B4900, which was completed by the end of November, was retained at the factory for experimental purposes. Deliveries of the next batch began the following January.

The Air Navigation Company delivered its first machines at the beginning of December, with C1751 was recorded as undergoing AID inspection on 5 December, while C1752 was at the Air Acceptance Park at Brooklands the previous day.

B700, last of a batch built by Vickers. It was transferred from one depot to another but appears never to have joined a squadron.

S.E.5a fuselages by Vickers' Works, Weybridge, on the finishing straight at Brooklands, after just one week's production. Such publicity shots, although not uncommon, must have required a lot of effort. (*Brooklands Museum*)

The Austin Motor Company delivered its first S.E.5a to the Air Acceptance Park at Coventry at the beginning of November 1917, with others following almost immediately; the batch of 350 was completed by June 1918. However, these production rates were not achieved easily, especially since the design was changed and new drawings were issued on what seemed to contractors to be an almost daily basis. Many, or indeed most of these modifications were quite small, and included such things as changing the radiator drain tap, changing the position of the splice in the aileron cable, and the addition of an engine speed-warning plate. The engine decelerator, which had been added to the control column following A4562's service trials at St Omer, but which had found no use in practice, was modified on 16 June, and then finally removed altogether on 29 September.

Each change meant some delay to production, and yet contractors were instructed to make a total of 100 changes in the six months between 6 June and 6 December 1917. Contractors had had more than enough, and on 22 December, the Austin Motor Company's eponymous founder, Sir Herbert Austin, complained to the Department of Aeronautical Supplies, which placed and oversaw production contracts. Austin stated:

> I am also enclosing a list of alterations made in the S.E.5 plane. These are even more important in comparison, and today we cannot foresee what is likely to happen at the end of next week, as we are waiting for drawings and instructions after the 128th machine, and we have already put the 110th into the erecting sheds.

The letter was forwarded to the recently appointed director general of aircraft production Sir William Weir, who made some effort to reduce the rate at which modifications were introduced. However, by the end of 1917, at total of 728 machines had been delivered, with a further 1,540 yet to be built to complete contracts already in place by that date.

One modification that was allowed to be introduced arose as the result of a complaint made by Major Bloomfield, commanding 56 Squadron, who on 13 July 1917, had written to complain that the undercarriages fitted to the S.E.5s frequently collapsed on landing. As a result, the Royal Aircraft Factory designed a new wooden undercarriage, the front leg of which was a narrow inverted 'Y' shape, with the axle moving upwards within the fork of the leg to absorb landing shocks. Officially known as the 'three strut undercarriage', it became known more simply as the 'wooden undercarriage', and was first introduced towards the end of the Royal Aircraft Factory's production batch B4841-4900. It was tested first on B4875, and was fitted to B4897 when that machine was presented for inspection on 15 November 1917.

On 18 January 1918, service pilot Lt Huxley of 68 Squadron reported that he found it to be 'a great improvement. It will stand rough usage and not wear out the bungee so quickly. It will give the pilots confidence.' It was therefore adopted as standard in the spring of 1918 with contractors being instructed to fit it as follows:

S.E.5as under construction at Austin's Works in March 1918.

Austin from their 251st machine (B8481); the Air Navigation Company from their 75th (C1823); Martyinsyde from their 201st (D3911); Vickers, Weybridge, from their 601st (D5951); Vickers, Crayford, from their 301st (D8431); and Wolseley from their 151st (D6851). Many of these machines represented the start of new contract batches, hopefully lessening the impact of the change upon production, and all were scheduled for delivery in late March or early April 1918.

On 19 March, the officer commanding the RFC's 2nd Brigade wrote to RFC headquarters:

> The supply of wooden undercarriages for S.E.5 machines is very poor, and a great difficulty is experienced in obtaining them. The steel tube type undercarriages are continually collapsing, and when this happens, the lower planes of the machine are nearly always damaged, necessitating a considerable amount of extra work.
>
> All squadrons in 2nd Brigade are experiencing this trouble, can something be done to hasten the supply of these wooden undercarriages.

Evidently something was done, for on 22 April, Brig.-Gen. Brooke-Popham instructed depots No. 1 and 2 that the wooden undercarriage was to be fitted to all S.E.5s received by them for overhaul. However, the entry of America into the war and the initiation of her own massive aircraft building programme had caused problems with the supply of timber for aircraft production, since much of it came from America. As a result, alternatives, especially varieties of cypress, were substituted for spruce or ash wherever possible. This material was widely used for building works throughout the southern states of America, and although on paper it was an adequate substitute, it proved less suitable in practice and eventually had to be largely withdrawn; the government bought up stocks held by aeroplane manufacturers who had bought it in response to official instructions and were now unable to use it. Thus on 13 May 1918, the director of aeronautical equipment was obliged to write to the officer commanding the Royal Air Force (which had come into existence on 1 April):

> I am to inform you that owing to the use of red cypress wood in wooden undercarriages for the S.E.5, and that this use has had to be discontinued, it has been necessary to authorise the issue of a considerable number of S.E.5s fitted with the metal undercarriage.

Most, if not all of these were eventually replaced with the wooden undercarriages, which remained standard for the rest of the S.E.5's existence.

Although the S.E.5 was justly praised for the speed at which it could dive, it was found that during this manoeuvre, it was possible for the leading edge of the fin to distort and appear 'like a sail blown out by the wind'. The solution was to fit an additional bracing wire from the existing attachment fitting on the tailplane spar

B4897, built by the Royal Aircraft Factory, was one of the first to be fitted with the wooden undercarriage.

An unusual angle, which shows the shape of the wing tips and tailplane.

to mid-point on the fin. This was done at the depots not only to all aircraft arriving from England for assignment to the squadrons, but also to any machine returned for repair or overhaul. Martinsyde Ltd modified the design of the fin fitted to all S.E.5as manufactured in their works from B61 onwards, which was completed in mid-November 1917, by including an additional vertical member at mid-chord. This greatly increased the strength of the fin and rendered the additional bracing wires unnecessary, although the depots fitted them anyway.

However, the high-speed dive was still not free of problems. On 4 January 1918, the starboard wing of C5334 broke up during a diving attack on an enemy aircraft, killing its pilot, the same Frederick Selous, by now promoted to captain, who had test flown the prototype at St Omer. A similar failure may have been responsible for the death of 2/Lt H. E. Barwell; on 3 February 1918, the starboard wing of B41 collapsed during a steep bank and the machine spun down from 2,000 feet to crash on its base airfield. The solution was to strengthen the box rib at the aileron cut-out, and to omit the routing of the rear spar for 6 inches either side of the attachment of that rib. The ribs aft of the rear spar were also stiffened. These modifications were introduced by Austin from B8477 onwards, by the Air Navigation Co. from C1813, by Wolseley from C6461, and by Vickers Crayford and Weybridge works from D330 and D3501 respectively. Remarkably, these accidents appear to have had no adverse effect on the S.E.5's enduring reputation for rugged strength and sound construction.

8

SQUADRON SERVICE

Capt. James McCudden, whose score then stood at six, joined 56 Squadron as a flight commander in August, having visited and even flown with the squadron in late June. He would score the remainder of his fifty-seven victories while flying with the squadron. Arthur Rhys-Davids was credited with twenty-three combat victories between May and 27 October 1917, when he too was shot down.

Another star pilot with 56 Squadron was Lt Leonard M. Barlow, who achieved twenty victories by 1 October when he was posted back to England for a rest, having shot down the first – a two-seater that crashed near Bellevue – on 24 April while flying A4858. Barlow crashed this aircraft near Lympne on 21 June during the squadron's temporary move to Bekesbourne, on the outskirts of Canterbury, for home defence duties. It was replaced by B507, in which Barlow scored at least seven victories before this machine was crashed by Rhys-Davids, after which it was returned to the depot for repair. Barlow then took over B511, scoring at least five further victories in it.

Many other 56 Squadron pilots reached high scores, for example, Lt Crowe was credited with having brought down fifteen enemy aircraft between April and July.

In the morning of 23 December 1917, McCudden encountered a patrol of four enemy Scouts and succeeded in bringing two of them down. In the afternoon, the patrol he was leading got into a dogfight with a flight of eight German Scouts, and two more fell to McCudden's guns.

An arrangement of twin Lewis guns, each on a Foster mount, was made to B4855 by 56 Squadron at the end of September 1917, but was not considered successful; the machine was sent to the depot for restoration to standard configuration.

56 had remained the only squadron operating the S.E.5/5a until July 1917, when sufficient machines were finally available to equip and maintain further squadrons. The second to receive the S.E.5a was 60 Squadron, which converted from the Nieuport 17 and 23, receiving its first S.E.5 from No. 1 Depot at St Omer on 8 July 1917, and the remainder shortly after. Its aircraft included A4853, A4856, A8918, and A8898, all of which had previously flown with 56 Squadron.

Close-up of the nose of an S.E.5a powered by a 200-hp geared Hispano-Suiza engine, showing the cylinder head fairings, rounded top radiator, and higher thrust line typical of the type.

A8898, in the rather colourful markings of 60 Squadron.

S.E.5as of 60 Squadron being prepared for take off.

A8898 suffered engine failure while taking off on 1 November 1917; its pilot, Lt A. Carter, was unhurt. A8898 returned to the depot for repair, and was later issued to 40 Squadron.

The Canadian William Avery 'Billy' Bishop, who had already been credited with an impressive tally of aircraft destroyed, served briefly with 60 Squadron before being sent home in August 1917, achieving eleven further victories while flying the S.E.5 with the squadron.

A8936, which joined 60 Squadron on 20 July, was flown by Bishop eight days later when he claimed an Albatros DIII, shot down in flames; it was the squadron's first S.E.5 victory. Bishop claimed a second Albatros DIII, out of control, the following day, when Capt. Keith Caldwell also scored with an Albatros driven down.

Initially based at Filescamp Farm, better known to RFC personnel at Le Hameau, 60 Squadron moved to St Marie Cappel on 7 September. Another ex-56 Squadron machine was B507, which arrived having been repaired after a crash on 10 September; it suffered engine failure while over the front on 5 October, and made a forced landing at the airfield occupied by Jasta 18. Its pilot 2/Lt J. J. Fitzgerald became a prisoner of war.

On 26 August, a query, originating with 60 Squadron, was raised regarding the aiming of the two guns of the S.E.5a. The brigade gunnery officer pointed out that if their muzzles were aligned parallel, the bullets at 200 yards would form two groups that would just overlap, giving the best possible spread. Brooke-Popham replied on behalf of the GOC that they were to be left converging, as designed, to get the greatest weight of bullets into the target area.

B507, which served with both 56 and 60 Squadrons, and was flown by Capt. Chidlaw-Roberts in the fight against Werner Voss. It is seen here after landing behind the lines due to engine failure.

Another 60 Squadron machine, B4897, before any squadron markings were applied.

On 23 September, a flight from 60 Squadron, including Capt. R. L. Chidlaw-Roberts, and Lt H. A. Hamersley, was returning from a patrol when the rearmost machine, Hamersley's, was attacked by a Fokker triplane. A patrol from 56 Squadron, led by McCudden in B4863, and including Capt. Reginald Hoidge and Lt Bowman, Lt V. P. Croyne, Lt Mayberry, Lt Muspratt, and Lt Rhys-Davids, was about to attack a group of Albatroses, but broke off and dived to the assistance of the 60 Squadron machines. Being short of petrol and believing that the odds were completely in 56 Squadron's favour, Chidlaw-Roberts, Cronyn, and Hamersley left them to it. Being slower than the S.E.s, both on the level and in a dive, and unable to benefit from its superior rate of climb as the S.E.s were already above it, the triplane had little choice, once attacked, other than to fight it out. The pilot was Werner Voss, and there followed one of the most famous dogfights of all time. Voss, using the manoeuvrability of his triplane to the full, fought for 10 minutes before his machine was hit first by Hoidge, then by Rhys-Davids, bringing it down. Keith Muspratt's S.E.5 was shot through the radiator and made a forced landing at 1 Squadron's airfield, while both Mayberry and Hoidge's machines were damaged, the former suffering further damage in the ensuing forced landing. Lt Cronyn had been flying A4563, the third prototype, which was also damaged, while Hamersley's S.E.5a was so badly damaged that it was considered not worth repairing. McCudden wrote of the fight:

> As long as I live I shall never forget my admiration for that German pilot, who single handedly fought seven of us for 10 minutes, and also put some bullets through all our machines. His flying was wonderful, his courage magnificent,

Typical early production S.E.5a, with a geared Hispano-Suiza engine, in service with the RFC in France.

and in my opinion he was the bravest German airman whom it has been my privilege to see fight.

Rhys-Davids simply said, 'I wish I could have brought him down alive.

On 20 November 1917, McCudden was on an offensive patrol between Gourancourt and Bourlin when he spotted an LVG two-seater and manoeuvred into position behind it. He fired both guns at it and its engine stopped, water streaming from its radiator. The LVG glided down to land to the south-east of Havincourt; the crew was taken prisoner by the 59th Division, and the machine, which was otherwise intact, was retained for examination.

84 Squadron, which had first formed up at Lilbourne in Northamptonshire, received its complement of S.E.5as during August 1917, including B556-561 and B564, all built by Vickers. It moved, ready to go into action, to Estree Blanche, a few miles south of St Omer, on 23 September, sharing the airfield with 56 Squadron, ready for the opening of the third battle of Ypres a few days later. One of its pilots was the South African Anthony Beauchamp-Proctor, who would score fifty-four victories flying the S.E.5a. He was barely over 5 feet tall, and had to have the seat and rudder bar of his machine modified so that he could maintain full control.

Sholto-Douglas, who was the squadron's commanding officer, later recalled how they preferred to attack:

> When we saw enemy aircraft approaching, we would climb as hard as we could, if possible up into the sun, and then would try to take them from above and behind, out of the sun. The superior performance of the S.E.5 allowed us to do this more or less with impunity.

He also recalled that the broad lap belt which secured the pilot in his seat allowed more freedom of movement, especially to look to the rear, than shoulder straps would have done, and that the cockpit never became warm in any weather.

The squadron was moved about the front, from battle to battle, and at the end of October, it was relocated to Izel-le-Hameau, west of Arras, ready for the Battle of Cambrai that took place in November and December. It moved again, to Flez, in the south of the British sector, before the end of the year. Among the aircraft that flew with the squadron was A4853, received on 22 October having been with both 56 and 60 Squadrons. B574, which joined 84 Squadron on 2 October 1917, was shot down less than two weeks later during a combat with the Albatroses from Jasta 15. Its pilot, 2/Lt T. V. Lord, became a prisoner of war.

40 Squadron, which after a period with Nieuports had been flying the pusher F.E.8, began converting to the S.E.5 in mid-October 1917; its first machines included A8913, which had previously served with 56 Squadron, and A8932, which had been with 60 Squadron. Other machines received included B13 and

Landing accidents were common, both in services and in training, with the typical result shown here. The damage, if not too serious, would be repaired at the base by replacing broken parts. Otherwise the machine would be sent to the depot to be either rebuilt or scrapped.

An unidentified helmeted pilot in his S.E.5a. (*R. B. Pope*)

B22 form the batch built by Martinsyde, B598 built by Vickers, and B4879 and 4881, both form the Royal Aircraft Factory, all arriving on 11 October. B587 and B589 followed three days later, with B20 and B24 being received on 15 October.

The squadron completed the changeover in just two weeks, and began operations at the end of the month, their first victory coming almost immediately with Lt W. MacLanachan sending a two-seater out of control on 31 October. He would score again on 12 November, while Lt L. A. Herbert brought down another two-seater ten days later. MacLanachan, incidentally, was usually known as 'McScotch' to distinguish him from the squadron's other 'Mac', Dublin-born George McElroy, or 'McIrish'.

41 Squadron, based at Lealvilliers, to the north-west of Albert on the Somme, received its first S.E.5a, B581, on 18 October 1917, in exchange for a DH5 that had been returned to the depot for overhaul. This prompted some pilots to make deliberately bad landings in order to make their own DH5s eligible for a similar exchange. The squadron got B628 on 27 October, B632 the following day, and B624 the day after that. At least five S.E.5as arrived on 7 November when the changeover began in earnest, with more being received the following week. The squadron was fully equipped and operational before the end of the month.

After the squadron's CO Major Frederick Powell was shot down and captured, Geoffrey Bowman transferred from 56 Squadron to take over command. He requested permission to take his current mount C9533 with him, and was allowed to do so provided that a 41 Squadron machine was sent back in exchange. B628 was selected. 41 Squadron also initiated a proposal that the Lewis gun should be removed and twin Vickers guns fitted instead. They carried out an experimental installation, but this was not approved, possibly because the fuselage was too narrow to accommodate the arrangement, or because, as with the converging of the muzzles, the RFC high command were satisfied with the armament as designed.

By the end of 1917, there were still only five RFC squadrons operating the S.E.5a in France. Although 32 Squadron began converting to the type before the end of the year, they would not be fully operational until well into the new year.

9

ENGINE TROUBLE

In order to obtain the maximum possible performance, the 200-hp geared engine was standardised for production aircraft on 11 July 1917, the depots also being instructed that any machines with the 150-hp engine brought in for overhaul should be fitted with the 200-hp version before being returned to service. However, the extreme reliability demonstrated by the 150-hp Hispano-Suiza V8 while under acceptance tests during 1915 unfortunately did not appear to carry over into the 200-hp version, at least not those built under licence by contractors. The increase in output was obtained at the expense of a disproportionate increase in the consumption of both oil and petrol. Oil leaks became common, as did fuel leaks and water leaks, from both the engine block and from the radiator, while problems with the reduction gears and uneven running due to the use of poor quality petrol caused the CC gear to malfunction, bullets then hitting the propeller with obvious consequences.

Engines built in France not only had different propeller bosses to those made in England, but also had differing reduction gear ratios, some retaining the original 24:41, others having 21:28 (1,500 rpm), or 26:39 (1,333 rpm). Crank pin lengths and diameters varied between different manufacturers, as did gear housing design, and of course, propeller type.

The version built by Wolseley Motors, the Adder, differed from the original design in having a compression ratio of 4.8:1 and a 35:59 reduction gear, which gave a propeller speed of 1,185 rpm, and used the same T28096 four-blade propeller as the 1,170-rpm version. However, tests had shown that a two-blade propeller gave better handling, creating less torque reaction during manoeuvres. B536, which was fitted with a 21:28 (1,500-rpm) geared engine manufactured by Delaunay-Belleville and a type T.28134 propeller, was tested by 60 Squadron, with which it was serving, on 10 October 1917. In a report that implies this was a new propeller and that the squadron was accustomed to the four-blade type, they stated:

An S.E.5a with the four-blade propeller associated with the 1,170-rpm geared engine.

Propeller seems satisfactory in every way, very remarkably so as regards the handiness of the machine. The improved handiness is very noticeable indeed, there being none of the very considerable torque, which is experienced with the four-blade propeller. With a four-blade propeller, an India rubber shock absorber had to be fitted to the rudder bar, the torque to be counteracted was so considerable. With the two-blade propeller, the torque is hardly noticeable at all in flying straight. In consequence, in turning at higher altitude, there is none of the tendency to spin as experienced with the ordinary 200-hp S.E.5.

The Wolseley Adder, when submitted for acceptance tests on 7 May 1917, was not an immediate success; the crankshaft broke after only about 4 hours running. After four successive crankshafts had failed under test, it was clear that steps had to be taken; as a stop-gap measure, the crankshaft webs were machined down and the engine was accepted for use with its rotational speed limited to a maximum of 1,750 rpm instead of the design speed of 2,000 rpm. At least two S.E.5as, A8923 and A8924, were handed over for active service with the limited speed engines.

With the Adder clearly needing further development, Wolseley was ordered to manufacture 400 direct-drive engines to fill the immediate need to power the

S.E.5. It was intended that these should the original 150-hp version, the 8Aa, which was known to be reliable, but the order was obviously not clear in its intent, and Wolseley set about modifying the design to provide a reliable 200 hp. The resulting engine would ultimately provide the solution to all the engine problems, but initially, completion of what should have been a straightforward order was delayed, and of the 400 engines expected by the end of August 1917, only ten had been delivered.

The Sunbeam Arab, a V8 engine of similar configuration and swept volume as the Hispano-Suiza, but of an otherwise completely different design, was considered as a possible alternative. One was fitted to B4900 by 24 November 1917, and a second to B4898 by 2 January 1918, with it going to Martlesham Heath on 25 January where it remained until 17 February. Sunbeam Arabs were also installed in a number of other machines, including B609, C1111 (which was tested with both geared and direct drive versions), D7017, and E1368, but all proved to be plagued with poor reliability and excessive vibration, and most orders for manufacture of the Arab, which had been ordered into production both from Sunbeam and a number of sub-contractors before development was complete, were therefore cancelled.

Meanwhile, the engines built by Brasier, when delivered, turned out to have problems of their own. The gears were imperfectly hardened and frequently failing; a problem exacerbated by poor quality petrol, which caused uneven firing, thereby placing a further strain on the gears. Brasier seem to have been unable to address the problem, and eventually these engines were all sent to the Clement Talbot Factory for the problems to be rectified. However, their reputation for reliability remained irrevocably and justifiably tarnished, so much so that Brig.-Gen. Brooke-Popham instructed the depots, 'When 1,170 S.E.5s are allotted, please issue any other 1,170 S.E.5 in preference to a Brasier. Brasier engines will only be issued to squadrons when no other 1,170 S.E.5 is available.'

Yet issued they most certainly were, for in the autumn of 1917, in what can only have been an act of extreme desperation, aeroplane engines with the faulty reduction gearing were issued for use, since, as the official history *The War in the Air* explained, 'Engines of incomplete efficiency were better than none at all.'

In order to achieve some degree of uniformity and thus simplify the issue of spares, 1,170-rpm engines were issued only to 24 and 56 Squadrons from 18 January 1918, with 1,500-rpm engines going to all other squadrons in France operating the S.E.5a.

As a result of these various problems, airframe manufacture easily outpaced that of the engines necessary to power them, even though many orders originally placed by the Admiralty for use by the RNAS now came under the control of the Ministry of Munitions and were allocated as required. As a result, many otherwise completed aircraft had to be delivered in crates without engines in order to complete contracts and secure payment. By the beginning of 1918, almost half of

Another S.E.5a fitted with the 1,170-rpm geared engine. The location is unknown but the presence of three B.E.2es in the background suggests either a shared airfield or a training establishment.

the machines manufactured to date were stored, awaiting engines. These machines were completed and issued as soon as engines became available, but with airframe manufacture continuing to outstrip that of engines, up to 400 engineless airframes were stored at any one time. On 5 February, for example, records show the number of engineless S.E.5s as 349, the number diminishing as engine production caught up with that of airframes.

These problems affected not only the S.E.5a, but other aircraft designed to have the 200-hp Hispano-Suiza engine too, such as the Sopwith Dolphin and SPAD XIII, and so further limited the availability of sufficient engines. The solution, at least as far as the S.E.5a was concerned, ultimately lay with the Wolseley direct-drive engine, the W4a Viper that had an increased compression ratio, a balanced crankshaft, and numerous other modifications, which gave a reliable 200 hp. The first installation was made in B4862, which had been completed on 16 August 1917 with a Wolseley Adder (No. 885/2233/WD8460), but which by 24 August had been fitted instead with a prototype Viper (although the engine had yet to be so named) No. 717/2233/WD8292.

The next day, following testing at the Royal Aircraft Factory, it was flown to Martlesham Heath where it was to remain for about six weeks, subjected to extensive testing. It was initially fitted with pistons giving a compression ratio of 5.68:1, then with pistons with lower crowns, reducing the compression to 5.3.

B4899 was fitted with the first production Viper engine. It is seen here later in its career, having acquired a wooden undercarriage.

After 15 hours running, the higher compression pistons were refitted for a further 12 hours running. The 5.3:1 compression ratio was judged superior and became the standard for production.

On 25 November 1917, B4899, fitted with a production Wolseley Viper No. A21777/WD1877, went to Martlesham Heath for further testing, and although some teething troubles still needed to be resolved, the Viper was considered satisfactory and was selected for all 1918 S.E.5a contracts.

Vipers were fitted without the small fairings to the projecting cylinder heads that distinguished all variants of the Hispano-Suiza, and although they initially had a one-piece radiator with a semi-circular top and full-length shutters, similar in appearance to that of the Hispano-Suiza, a new, distinctive design specific to the Viper was soon developed and standardised for the Viper engine. This had two separate blocks, arranged vertically on either side of the propeller shaft and connected at the top with a header tank, which had a straight top with slightly angled shoulders. Separate sets of shutters were fitted to each block, although they operated together.

Radiators had long been a problem with the S.E.5, and in September 1917, the indefatigable Brig.-Gen. Brooke-Popham had informed the director of aeronautical equipment that at any given moment, one in seven of the S.E.5s on active service in France was out of action due to a leaking radiator. The solution appears to have been to replace the cellular film radiator core with the more expensive, but more reliable, honeycomb type.

The high thrust line and two-blade propeller of the faster turning geared Hispano-Suiza engines is clearly illustrated in this unidentified example.

A detail of the cockpit area showing the streamlined blocks used to raise the foster mounting when a geared engine was fitted.

B4862 fitted with an underslung radiator comprised of two Viper radiator blocks mounted horizontally.

However, the problem did not end there, as there were several different types of single-block radiator in use, and on 5 March 1918, the depots were instructed to issue S.E.5as to squadrons in accordance with the type of radiator fitted in order to maintain the same type throughout each squadron.

It was found that three different methods of fitting the Wolseley Viper and its cooling system had somehow evolved, with both No. 2 Depot and the Southern Aeroplane Repair Depot, which was building S.E.5as from spares recovered from damaged machines, having devised their own in addition to that designed at the Royal Aircraft Factory. Each was evaluated and assessed, and on 10 April, an instruction was issued that the factory designs should be followed for all future installations, ensuring that all S.E.5as would be broadly similar, with a wooden undercarriage, a Viper engine, and a twin-block radiator with full height shutters.

An experiment was conducted in which the frontal radiator of B4862 was removed, the nose being faired to a blunt shape with rounded edges, and an underslung radiator, comprising two standard Viper type radiator blocks mounted horizontally, was fitted beneath the forward fuselage. Tested at Martlesham Heath on 30 January 1918, it was found that speed at 15,000 feet was reduced by up to 14 mph while taking 5 minutes longer to climb to that altitude. The idea was obviously not adopted.

10

TRAINING

Almost as soon as the S.E.5 first entered squadron service, examples were assigned to training units. A4849, from the Royal Aircraft Factory's first production batch, went without engine or armament as a ground instruction airframe to the School of Technical Training at Reading, the training of ground engineers being at least as important as that of pilots.

However, pilots were not forgotten; the Central Flying School received its first S.E.5 A8915 in June 1917, with others from the same batch, including A8916, A8917, and A8926. A8927 later joined it. A8941 joined CFS on 28 July 1917 after a brief career in home defence.

A8927 was lost on 27 August 1917 when it spun shortly after take off. The pilot, 2/Lt F. M. Wood, was killed. Casualties in training were high for a variety of reasons, one of which was the lack of machines, even basic trainers, with dual controls.

By the middle of the war, flying training had become rather more comprehensive than before. Novice pilots were required to have made a cross-county flight of at least 60 miles, including landing at an airfield other than their base, to have reached a height in excess of 6,000 feet, and to have flown at least 15 hours solo, although these requirements were occasionally relaxed a little in times of heavy losses to maintain the RFC's policy of not having empty seats in the mess. Where possible, at least some of their solo hours were expected to have been on a front-line type, but for most pilots, these were obsolescent types that had already been superseded for front-line duties.

A typical training programme experienced by one pilot who qualified in June 1918 was 4 hours dual instruction in a two-seat trainer before going solo, then after about 30 hours experience, some time on a more advanced type, in this case a Sopwith Pup, followed by a week's course at a School of Gunnery and Aerial Fighting. He was then posted to a front-line squadron where he was allowed 8 hours of practice behind the lines on a S.E.5a before his first operational patrol.

B4870, which
served at
28 Training
Squadron
at Castle
Bromwich.
It brushed a
tree top on
10 December
1917, the
results of which
can be seen.

D8434 with
47 TDS at
Doncaster, with
a mechanic in
rather unusual
headgear.

F5609 with
the Central
Flying School at
Upavon.

B18 after conversion into a two-seat trainer. The new front cockpit has full instrumentation, but access to it must have been difficult.

Only when production had satisfied the demands of active service did current designs, such as the S.E.5a, find their way to training squadrons. Thus, 6 Training Squadron eventually received D251 and D415, 10 Training Squadron at Lilbourne got D401, and E5891 went to 74 Reserve Squadron at Castle Bromwich. 93 Squadron, based at Chattis Hill, received its first S.E.5a in January 1918. William Lambert, who was to become America's second highest scoring pilot of the war, was with the squadron for advanced training. He later recalled, 'The cockpit fitted me like a new glove; all controls, switches and so on were well within close reach for any quick action. The stick and rudder bar had been made for me. Right then and there I decided that this was the aeroplane I was going to fly.'

Making his first flight in the S.E.5a, a 1,170-rpm model with a four-blade propeller, on 31 January 1918, Lambert found, 'It would roll, spin, climb, loop, and dive at the least touch of the stick and rudder bar, and was under perfect control at all times.'

However, not all pilots took to flying a front-line Scout so easily, but the problem of giving dual instruction to pilots converting to the S.E.5a from more basic types was resolved early in 1918 when the Central Flying School devised a two-seat conversion. The armament was removed, and the main petrol tank was drastically reduced in size to a capacity of just 12 gallons, so that a second cockpit could be fitted ahead of the original. Conversion of B18 was completed by 17 March, and

Aircraft of 6 Training Squadron Australian Flying Corps, based at Minchinhampton.

Another view of 6 Squadron AFC at Minchinhampton.

F912 at Hucknall with a number of ground crew in attendance. The machine in the background is a Bristol F2b Fighter.

F5696 at CFS. It is fitted with a Hythe camera gun on the Foster mounting for gunnery training.

although the performance and handling were somewhat adversely affected by the change, the advantages of being able to offer dual instruction were so great that a number of other machines were converted.

On 26 September 1918, the director of aeronautical equipment informed the general officer commanding the Royal Air Force that, 'In addition to normal work of the depots in this country, [we] have now been called upon to convert a very large number of machines for training purposes from single to two-seater machines in order that they may be used with dual control.'

Having learned to fly the S.E.5a, it was then necessary, or at least desirable, that pilots should learn to fight in it; for this purpose, schools of aerial fighting and gunnery were eventually established. B660, C5323, and D3432 were all assigned to No.1 School of Aerial Fighting based at Ayr. E5544 was among the S.E.5as at No. 2 School, and D3518 was shipped to the school based at Heliopolis in Egypt.

D411 also went to No. 1 School, where in an accident that was unusual even for a training unit, it collided with Avro 504, D7583. At 6 Squadron AFC, a training unit based at Minchinhampton, an equally unusual accident occurred on 28 July 1918 when D415 ran into a hangar on landing, ending up on its nose, causing slight injury and no doubt a great deal of embarrassment to its pilot Lt H. W. Miller.

Casualties in training were almost as numerous as those in action on the Western Front, although the S.E.5a proved far safer than its major rival; accidents in S.Es accounted for just 2.5 per cent of the RFC's total casualties. The figure for the tricky Sopwith Camel was over six times greater.

Other training units also eventually received examples of the S.E.5a, occasionally after they had been with an operational unit and perhaps deemed unfit for further active service. Thus, after a period with 61 Squadron on home defence duties, B672 was sent to the Officers' School of Technical Training at Henley-on-Thames. As production finally caught up with demand, more S.E.5as went directly to training units; for example, F5277, F5609, F5636, and F5696 all went to the CFS at Upavon immediately after acceptance. F5696 was one of many training machines fitted with a Hythe camera gun. These, manufactured by Thornton-Pickard, closely resembled the Lewis gun; used in mock combat, they recorded any hits by photographing the aiming point when the trigger was pressed.

11

HOME DEFENCE

Shortly after 11.00 a.m. on Thursday 13 June 1917, a force of about fifteen German Gotha bombers crossed the English coast near Broadstairs in Kent and headed for London, dropping their bombs on the East End. Britain's defences proved powerless to stop them. The aeroplanes of the home defence squadrons, stationed at intervals along the east coast, had proved effective against the Zeppelins that had raided by night, but this new enemy flew at heights greater than many of them could even reach. Nor did the anti-aircraft guns manage to hit any of the raiders. Casualties among the largely unprepared civilian population amounted to 104 people killed and 423 injured, a huge number for the time, and one that included 120 children, one of the buildings bombed having been a school. No military or naval buildings or installations were hit.

The public reaction was immediate; there was a clamour for reprisal raids against Germany and for better defences for London. As *The Times* reported the next day, 'Two questions were much discussed yesterday. One was why our system of defence failed to protect the city, and the other why the authorities do not take steps to notify the public of the approach of hostile aircraft.'

Parliament debated the issue over the next few days, noting the rising public outcry, and decided that the current warning system, which largely comprised of telephone calls to military bases, would be extended to give public warning of air raids. They also decided that London's defences should be strengthened by recalling an experienced fighter squadron from France to be stationed on the approaches to London. The squadron chosen was 56, then still the only squadron equipped with the S.E.5, the fastest and best-armed machine available. Whether this was intended as a serious attempt to provide a proper fighter defence, or merely a gesture to appease public opinion is unclear, but whatever the reason, on 21 June, the squadron returned to England, landing at Bekesbourne near Canterbury, although Lt Barlow force landed A4598 at Lympne due to engine failure. The next day, 'A' flight was detached to Rochford, just north of Southend, to cover the north side of the Thames estuary, the most obvious route into London.

Lt Arthur Rhys Davids of 56 Squadron, seated in his S.E.5 while at Bekesbourne in July 1917.

S.E.5a A8940 of 56 Squadron at Bekesbourne, July 1917.

While awaiting another air raid, the pilots of 56 Squadron seem to have enjoyed a comparative rest, spending their evenings enjoying dinners, dances, and occasional trips to 'town'. It was during this stay in England that McCudden first visited the squadron and resolved to join it.

No further raids occurred, and on 5 July, the squadron flew back to France, landing at Estree Blanche at about 5.00 p.m., ready to resume their normal duties.

On 7 July, twenty-one Gothas again raided London, suggesting either very good luck or superb intelligence; one of them took a photograph of an area of London, including St Paul's cathedral, from 14,000 feet. This time, the raid caused fewer casualties, largely because an elaborate system of communication had been set up to give warning of the raiders' approach. By now, 39 Squadron, based at Suttons Farm to the east of London, had been allocated three S.E.5as – A8924, A8939, and A8941 – and had begun anti-Gotha patrols on 4 July, before 56 Squadron's return to France. On the day of the raid, 7 July, patrols were flown by at least two S.Es, A8941 being flown by Lt E. S. Moulton-Barrett, and the other machine returning early with engine problems. Neither engaged, or even saw the raiders.

The allocation of these three machines to 39 Squadron appears to have been a stop-gap measure, and by the end of the month, A8941 had been re-assigned to the Central Flying School, although the other two continued on home defence duties.

An experimental installation of three Lewis guns, originally devised by Capt. E. Eeman of the Weaponry Experimental Unit at Orford Ness, was fitted to B4875. This appears to have been devised as a method of countering the downward-firing gun that the Gotha bombers were thought to possess to protect their tails. The guns were angled upwards at 45 degrees to the horizontal, the bullet's trajectory being straight for about 600 to 800 yards before loss of velocity allowed gravity to take effect. B4875 was completed in mid-September 1917, and by October, had been extensively modified to accommodate the unusual armament. The gravity tank was moved to the starboard wing, and a new centre section added, with three slots in a 'Y' formation for the gun muzzles. The cockpit arrangement was also modified; some instruments were repositioned to make space for the gun breeches and a transparent panel was fitted in the fuselage side. Martlesham Heath expected to receive the machine for testing by December 1917, but even as late as 9 February 1918 it had not arrived, and no evidence has been found of its ever doing so. This suggests that the German bombers had been found not to be as formidably armed as first thought, and the idea had been quietly abandoned.

The daylight raids by Gothas were not the only attacks upon England, with night raids both by airships and aeroplanes occurring with sufficient regularity to cause the population sleepless nights, both literally and figuratively. Therefore in December 1917, the S.E.5 was formally assessed for night flying, being considered easy to fly and with a large margin of performance over the enemy bombers. Its

B554 served with a home defence unit but was never fitted out for night flying.

one disadvantage, compared to rotary-powered machines such as the Sopwith Pup and Camel, was the time needed for its engine to warm up before take off, reducing its suitability as an interceptor fighter.

In response to daylight raids, the RFC rightly sent every available aeroplane up to try to engage the enemy, but night raids were a different matter, with a risk that the defending machines might collide in the dark. A system of patrols was established, with each aircraft having an assigned height and patrol path. The aircraft were fitted with a Holt flare mounted on the wing tip to facilitate landing at night on unmarked fields, as well as small lamps over the instruments. These were fitted by squadron mechanics as soon as the machines were received from the depot, and their use as night fighters was thus established.

61 Squadron, based at Rochford, and so on the eastern approaches to London, had been equipped with Sopwith Pups and formed as a home defence unit in August 1917. It began conversion to the S.E.5a in November when B655 arrived, and was in action by the middle of December. On the night of 18/19 December, when German bombers raided London, at least four patrols were flown, their times overlapping. The aircraft involved were B655, flown by Capt. Mason, B679 (Lt P. Thompson), C1051, and C9406 flown by Capt. C. Lewis.

Lt Lionel Blaxland, who joined 61 Squadron after serving in France with 40 Squadron, recalled some fifty years later, 'I found the S.E.5a a difficult machine to land at night, mainly due to the flashes from the exhaust pipes as the engine was

Capt. Stroud of 61 Squadron posing by his S.E.5a, which is fitted with flame dampers and an unusual steel tube undercarriage.

throttled back for landing.' Other pilots found the same difficulty; Lt G. C. Young, a Canadian pilot with 61 Squadron, therefore devised a flame damper that fitted over the discharge ports of the exhaust, eliminating the problem. The dampers appear to have been first fitted to D3459, which later also served with 37 Squadron at Stow Maries, and their use became fairly widespread among night flying S.E.5as.

On the night of 29/30 January 1918, Blaxland took off in C1756, but returned with engine trouble; he transferred to C1062, but returned after 1.00 a.m., again having seen nothing. However, despite this lack of contact with the enemy, he regarded his time on home defence as 'every bit as important as the work in France'.

A number of 61 Squadron aircraft, including B658 and C1061, were painted all over with a diamond pattern by over-painting the normal PC10 finish with another colour, possibly grey. This was of course not visible when flying at night, and on the night of 17/18 February 1918, B658 was hit by 'friendly fire' from the anti-aircraft battery at Benfleet, near to its base at Rochford. Fortunately, damage was limited to a few holes, none of them in the pilot Capt. C. A. Lewis, formerly of 56 Squadron, who had been transferred to home establishment for a 'rest'. The aircraft was quickly repaired and back in service. By 26 April, it had been transferred to 37 Squadron, which operated a few S.E.5as as a detached flight at Stow Maries in Essex, but crashed on 22 May 1918 while attempting a turn close to the ground with a failing engine. The pilot, 2/Lt W. Burfoot, was killed. D3459 also moved from 61 Squadron to 37, retaining its diamond pattern markings.

D5995 of 50 Squadron at Bekesbourne sometime in 1918. The occupant of the cockpit is believed to be Lt L. Lucas.

50 Squadron also had a detached flight at Bekesbourne equipped with S.E.5as, including D5995. 143 Squadron, formed in February 1918, also operated in the home defence role and was based from March at Detling near Maidstone in Kent, where it received a batch of Royal Aircraft Factory-built S.E.5as – C1801-1810 – all powered by the Wolseley Viper direct-drive engine.

The last major raid on London by German bombers took place on the night of 18/19 May 1918, with almost all the home defence squadrons flying patrols to try to engage the raiders.

With the threat to the nation's capital over, 89 Squadron, which had been formed at Catterick in July 1917 in response to the Gotha raids, moved to Harling Road, Norfolk, in August, and was disbanded on 29 July 1918. Its S.E.5as were re-allocated to other squadrons. At least of one of them, E1386, which went to 29 Squadron, achieved a combat victory in France.

94 Squadron, which had also been based at Harling Road, was re-mobilised as a Scout squadron and moved to France, taking many of its S.E.5as with it. Since it did not commence active service until 2 November 1918, its aircraft saw little or no action. However, one of its former machines, F863, which had been re-allocated to 56 Squadron when 94 Squadron re-mobilised, was flown by Capt. D. Grinell-Milne for the remainder of the war, bringing down three Fokker DVIIs.

12

EXPERIMENTAL MODIFICATIONS

Before, and even after the S.E.5a had reached a more or less standard pattern, experiments to improve various aspects of its performance, especially with regard to control, continued. A number of S.E.5as built by the Royal Aircraft Factory, including B4890 and B4891, were fitted with elevators of reduced area, their chord being 10 inches instead of 15. Both of these machines served with 56 Squadron, the latter being flown by McCudden, who scored a number of victories in it before it force landed on 21 March 1918, when Major C. M. Crowe, who was flying it at the time, ran out of petrol. Two days later, it was returned to No. 2 Depot at Candas. A number of machines of the Royal Aircraft Factory's third production batch (A8898-A8947) were completed with the reduced chord elevators. These appear to have improved control, making the stick forces lighter, and reducing the need to adjust the trim. On 22 February 1918, the officer commanding the third RFC Brigade wrote to RFC headquarters requesting that they should be made standard for all future machines, but for some unexplained reason this was not done and the original elevators continued to be fitted.

Ailerons of reduced chord were also tried, presumably in attempt to improve the S.E.5's less than perfect lateral control. This was a more complicated modification than that of the elevators, requiring the provision of a false spar from which to hinge the ailerons. A4864 was thus modified, and was tested by the Royal Aircraft Factory with the narrow ailerons on 26 July 1917. It was also flown by a number of pilots of 56 Squadron, then in England on home defence duties. A8938 was also fitted with the reduced chord ailerons, the modification being completed by 18 September, and was taken to Martlesham Heath on 25 October, returning to Farnborough the following day. On 11 November, it crashed while being flown by Capt. G. T. R. Hill, but the damage was not serious and it was flying again, still with the small ailerons, by the end of the month.

Efforts to improve lateral control also led to C1063 being tested with reduced dihedral, presumably in the hope that reducing stability might increase manoeuvrability. It was rigged first with its dihedral reduced from 5 degrees to 2.5

E5927 after modification to its tail surfaces at Martlesham Heath.

and later to 0 degrees, but no advantage was gained. A number of service pilots also tried having their machines' dihedral reduced, but with a similar lack of any advantage.

Although no criticism had been made of the S.E.5s directional stability or control, a number of machines were fitted with modified vertical tail surfaces; A8938 had had a balanced rudder fitted by 15 July 1917. D203, which was built by Vickers and delivered towards the end of February 1918, was adopted by the Royal Aircraft Factory as a test vehicle. Almost immediately, it was fitted with a balanced rudder and modified fins with curved leading edges, the whole assembly being similar to that of the Sopwith Dolphin. In addition, it had the narrow chord ailerons, and was at some point rigged with reduced dihedral. On 9 March, it crashed while being flown by Major H. Tizard, who was unhurt. The aircraft appears not to have flown again until July, when it still had the balanced rudder. By 23 October, it had been further modified and now had twin fins as well as an Avro-type balanced rudder; later that month, it was flown in spinning tests. It was also fitted with a modified undercarriage with steel tube legs and a split axle. It was then fitted with twin fins and rudders as in drawing AD2653, in which the curved ventral fin employed with the Dolphin-type rudder was retained, and small fins with curved leading edges and rudders of a very rounded shape were fitted mid way along the span of each side of the tailplane. It was test flown as the modifications took place by a number of pilots, including Lt Colin, Flg Off. Scholefield, Flt Lt Candy, Flt Lt Noakes, and Squadron Leader Hill.

A8947 after conversion to the S.E.5b. The upper wing has been increased in size, the lower wing reduced, and the nose redesigned. Although it looks faster than the standard S.E.5a, it did not prove to be so.

The test report No. BA385, which was not finally published until 1 April 1921, stated that the machine would come out of a spin on its own when fitted with the standard vertical surfaces, but not when fitted with either the Avro or Dolphin types. The Avro rudder gave more pleasant control, but required larger movements to be effective, while the Dolphin type did not give the same maximum control. With the twin fins, it was found that it was only just possible to fly straight at 40 mph if full left rudder was applied, and tests with this arrangement were therefore discontinued. The report concluded that, 'For all round service flying, there is no doubt that the standard fin and rudder combination was not surpassed by any of the experimental ones.'

Presumably, the standard vertical surfaces were restored, as it was flying at Farnborough, testing various designs of exhaust manifolds, at least until November 1923.

By April 1918, A8947, which had been retained by the Royal Aircraft Factory where it had originally been built, and which had already been tested with narrow chord elevators, had been so extensively modified, it had almost become a new aeroplane, the S.E.5b. The original fuselage, tailplane, and undercarriage were retained, but the radiator was replaced with a retractable unit beneath the fuselage and the nose was rounded into a streamline shape. The Aries-built 200-hp Hispano-Suiza engine No. 10317/WD10171, with which the machine had originally been

The streamlined nose of the S.E.5b.

built, was refitted, having been removed while a high-compression version was tested. But it was without its reduction gear, probably to give a lower thrust line. A non-standard propeller, Etoile 34/765, was fitted, and provided with a large, rather shallow spinner that blended smoothly into the contours of the streamlined nose. The headrest fairing was extended further back along the fuselage and had a slightly curved top, adding to the streamlined appearance of the design.

The wing structure was entirely new, and the upper wing much larger than the lower to gain – it was hoped – the aerodynamic advantages of the sesquiplane, without the consequent loss of strength, as the lower wing retained two spars. The upper wing spanned a little over 30 feet and had a chord of 6 feet, while the lower span was some 4 feet shorter. Its chord was just 4 feet and 3 inches, and RAF15 section proved too thin to allow the use of spars of sufficient depth, and so a new, deeper section, RAF22, was developed specifically for it. Ailerons were fitted to the upper wing, hinged from false rear spars, and the interplane struts were raked outwards to pick the same relative points in each span.

The completed machine was submitted for inspection on 4 April 1918, approval being given four days later, when test flying began. It was hoped that both its speed and rate of climb would show an improvement over the standard S.E.5a, but in this its designers were disappointed, for the increased induced drag of the large upper wing offset any advantage given by the streamlining of the nose, and

The standard S.E.5a that was flown in comparison to the S.E.5b.

its performance was little different. Although its angle of glide was better with the radiator retracted, and engine cooling slightly better, the standard S.E.5a, fitted with a similar engine and propeller, proved superior in all other aspects of performance.

Its undercarriage was damaged on 3 May 1918 while it was being flown by Flt Lt Jack Noakes, but was flying again by 27 June. Later in 1918, it was refitted with standard wings – the streamlined nose being retained – and was flown in comparison with a standard S.E.5a, D7018, and another, E5923, the tail surfaces of which had been modified at Martlesham Heath. This aircraft had a triangular tailplane with inversely tapered elevators, a curved upper fin, the lower fin being unaltered, and a rounded balanced rudder; the whole tail assembly had a remarkably Germanic appearance. The tests were conducted at the Royal Aircraft Establishment (as the factory had been renamed to avoid a clash of initials with the Royal Air Force), whose report BA356 stated that modified tail surfaces gave an improvement in longitudinal control, but a decrease in stability, there being 'no evidence that the triangular shape had any advantage over the standard type of tailplane'.

The modified rudder compared unfavourably with the standard type, although elevator control was lighter. All three machines were judged as being similar to land, and all recovered from a spin in 600 and 700 feet. Roderic Hill flew the E5923 with its modified tail just once, and thought it better for cruising about, but as a service aeroplane, he considered it inferior in a general way. As a result, the design of the S.E.5 was unaltered, and British aeroplane designers retained the rectangular tailplane for the immediate future.

13

MOUNT OF ACES

As engine production caught up with that of airframes and the number of available machines increased, other squadrons converted to the S.E.5a. 24 Squadron received its first S.E.5a in the last days of 1917, and its personnel spent most of January familiarising themselves both with its new aircraft and a new airfield, moving to Villiers-Bretonneux early in the new year. At least one of its newly acquired S.E.5as, B8268, was damaged during this training period, when on 14 January, Lt C. H. Crosbee ran into a ditch on landing, smashing both the propeller and the radiator drain off cock. The squadron became operational again on 26 January, just in time to move again, this time to Metigny. One of the squadron's first replacement S.E.5as collected from the depot on 2 February was B548, which had been returned to the depot by 56 Squadron after suffering damage in combat. Unfortunately, its left-hand undercarriage collapsed on landing at Vert Galant. Quickly repaired on 26 February, it was one of a flight of four machines, led by Capt. G. E. H. McElroy, that was attacked from above by a mixed group of about a dozen enemy fighters. B548 was hit in the fuel tank, drenching the pilot's legs in petrol and stopping the engine. Unable to stretch the glide far enough to reach safety, the pilot Lt C. H. Crosbee landed near the German reserve trenches and was promptly taken prisoner.

McElroy had previously served with 40 Squadron, where he was nicknamed 'McIrish', arriving while it was still equipped with Nieuports, which didn't seem to suit him. His first victory did not come until 28 December 1917, soon after the squadron had converted to the S.E.5a. By the third week of February, when he was transferred to 24 Squadron as a flight commander, his tally had risen to eleven. He was brought down by ground fire on 31 July 1918, having achieved a score of forty-seven, making him Ireland's most successful fighter pilot of the war.

32 Squadron also received its first S.E.5a in December 1917, gradually replacing its DH5s, with the two very different types being operated side by side during the changeover. The first victory with the S.E.5a was an Albatros DV, which was shot down on 8 March. The squadron's star pilot was Capt. W. A. Tyrell, who having

B548, seen after its undercarriage collapsed on landing at Vert Galant on 2 February 1918. It was lost on 26 February and its pilot, Lt Crosbee, was taken prisoner. (*Colin Huston*)

achieved five victories with the DH5, added twelve more to his score flying B8374, before he was hit by small arms fire while carrying out a ground attack mission on 9 June 1918.

The first day of 1918 saw Edward 'Mick' Mannock, then a flight commander with 40 Squadron and already an established 'ace', bring down a DFW two-seater while flying B665 – his first victory with the S.E.5a. Later in the month, he was posted back to home establishment, but returned to France in March, joining 74 Squadron as a flight commander.

January 1918 also saw No.1 Squadron convert from the Nieuport to the S.E.5a, with Capt. P. J. Clayton scoring his first victory on 16 February. From May to July, he claimed twenty-one victories, eighteen of them while flying C1114. On 9 June, returning from an early patrol, three of 1 Squadron's S.E.5as, led by Clayton in C1114, were attacked by a similar number of Fokker triplanes, one of which was brought down during the ensuing combat, landing more or less intact on the Allied side of the lines. Credit was given to Lt J. C. Bateman in B8254, and the Fokker was taken away for examination as G/2Bde/15. Clayton returned to the UK for a rest at the end of July, and stayed on in the RAF after the war, his total of twenty-nine combat victories making him the highest scoring pilot to do so.

Another squadron that converted from DH5s to S.E.5as early in 1918 was 64 Squadron; their first combat victories with the S.E. was achieved on 8 March, when in one patrol, Capt. James Slater and Lt R. H. Topliss each sent a Pfalz DIII out of control. Later the same day, Slater and Lt Rose each claimed an Albatros.

32 Squadron on 6 April 1918. The censor has obliterated the serials and identity letters. The aircraft nearest the camera has had its cockpit sides cut down to improve elbow room.

Air Mechanics of 32 Squadron working on an S.E.5a in April 1918. The aircraft in the background are Sopwith Camels of 73 Squadron, which shared the same airfield at Humieres.

F871, built by Wolseley Motors, served with both 94 and 1 Squadrons. It is seen here with neither a Lewis gun nor an Aldis sight fitted. The additional wire, which braced the leading edge of the fin, can be clearly seen.

Slater scored again three days later, claiming another Albatros and a Pfalz, his score reaching twenty-two before he was rested at the end of May. The whole squadron did well on 23 March, when during the German advance, they achieved eight victories; but they bettered that record on 16 May, claiming nine Albatros DVs in a 10-minute dogfight over Brebieries. On 30 May, they claimed a total of twelve combat victories, eight destroyed and four out of control.

Capt. H. G. White of 29 Squadron, the last to operate the Nieuport 17, collected his squadron's first S.E.5a from the depot on 3 March 1918. Despite some difficulty, made worse by the need to move to a new airfield and a number of crashes, the changeover was completed by the middle of the following month, and the squadron returned to active service, with the last Nieuport being returned to the depot on 20 April. Success with the S.E.5a began on 15 May, when Capt. R. H. Rusby attacked a pair of German two-seaters, bringing one down. Two days later, Capt. White sent an enemy Scout down in flames. June brought a string of victories, the squadron engaging in combat on almost every patrol; it remained busy throughout the remainder of the war, flying its last patrol on 10 November when a large group of Fokker DVIIs was encountered and five victories were claimed.

The day of the creation of the Royal Air Force, amalgamating the RFC and RNAS, saw four S.E.5a pilots claim victories: Lt V. Glentworth of 32 Squadron; 2/Lt W. L. Harrison of 40 Squadron; Lt W. J. Duncan of 60 Squadron; and Capt. George McElroy ('McIrish'), then a flight commander with 24 Squadron. The

S.E.5as of 94 Squadron lined up including, from the left, F871, E6032, and F896, which survived the war and joined the civil register as G-EBFF.

crew dived on three enemy aircraft, firing from 100 yards and sending one of them down in a spin. On 7 April, McElroy attacked three enemy two-seaters, sending one down before going to the aid of three S.E.5as that were dogfighting with a larger formation of Fokker triplanes, aiding one of their number to his score. However, on coming in to land, he brushed a top of a tree and was sufficiently injured to be sent to hospital; upon his recovery, he returned to 40 Squadron.

Further squadrons converted to the S.E.5a throughout the remainder of the war, with 85 Squadron becoming fully equipped in April, and 37 Squadron in May. The pilots of 85 Squadron included the Americans Laurence Callahan, Elliot White Springs, and John McGavock Grider. On 17 June, the squadron claimed five victories in a single patrol, with the Commanding Officer 'Billy' Bishop shooting down three, Lt A. Cunningham-Reid another, and Lt J. D. Canning, Lt Springs, and Lt Grider sharing the fifth. The following day, Grider, in C1883, and Springs, in D6851, were flying an offensive patrol and engaged a two-seater near Menin, bringing it down. During the action, the two were separated, and Grider did not return. His diary was later published by Springs under the title *War Birds: The Diary of an Unknown Aviator*.

Bishop was not the only pilot to claim three victories in a single mission, although he did so on several occasions. On 17 June 1918, while flying C1904, he

All of 85 Squadron's eighteen S.E.5as lined up.

claimed an Albatros and two two-seaters, the first of them falling in flames. On 1 June 1918, Mannock, in D6488, engaged a formation of enemy Scouts, believed to be Pfalzs with dark coloured tails, attacking from the front and above. He fired first at the nearest machine, its lower wings falling away as it plummeted down to crash, then turned on a second machine, firing only a short burst at close range before it fell in flames. He then fired at a third machine, which quickly went down in a spin. All this was confirmed by other members of the patrol, and Mannock was credited with two aircraft destroyed and one out of control.

On occasion, other pilots did even better, with W. G. Claxton of 41 Squadron claiming six victories on 30 July, four in the morning and two more on an evening patrol. He scored a total of thirty-seven between 27 May and 17 August, when he was shot down flying F5910, and after a period in hospital, became a prisoner. F. R. G. McCall, also from 41 Squadron, was credited with a total of four victories while flying D3927 on 28 June, and five more just two days later.

Mannock took over command of 85 Squadron when Bishop was posted home at the end of June, scoring his first victory with the squadron on 8 July. His place as a flight commander with 74 Squadron was taken by Capt. J. I. T. Jones, who on 6 August was flying a lone patrol in D6958 when he spotted nine Fokker DVIIs and was able make his attack from the east, from where it would be least expected. However, he had to break off, as he had neglected to cock his guns, proving that even the most experienced pilot could make an occasional mistake. Next, he spotted a lone R.E.8 being attacked by two Fokkers and fired at them from 200 yards, hoping to distract them while the reconnaissance machine dived for the

Another line-up in which the censor has removed the serials but retained the code letters and squadron markings, which are those of 85 Squadron.

lines. The two German machines each turned to avoid his tracer, but collided and locked together. Jones fired again and the saw them go down in flames.

It was not uncommon for pilots to make minor changes to their machines to suit their individual taste. Broad-shouldered pilots occasionally had the sides of the cockpit either cut down or bulged out to provide more elbow room, and the headrest fairings were often removed to afford a slight improvement in the view to the rear. Some S.E.5as also had the exhaust pipes shortened and cut back to just aft of the manifold, although the reason, or any possible benefit, is unclear.

While a flight commander with 56 Squadron, McCudden fitted the propeller of his S.E.5a B4891 with a large red spinner recovered from a LVG CV two-seater that he had brought down on 30 November 1917. McCudden claimed that the spinner added 3 mph to the machine's top speed, although the result of tests on similar installations conducted by the Royal Aircraft Factory showed no similar improvement. B4891 was almost certainly the highest scoring machine of the war, with McCudden achieving thirty-one victories in it and other pilots adding several more.

McCudden was flying it in the morning of 16 February 1918 when he spotted a Rumpler two-seater climbing up over Caudry. Although on escort duties, he promptly attacked, sending it down in a vertical dive, during which all four wings were seen to fall off. 10 minutes later, he sent a DFW down in flames, and while watching its descent, his machine was hit by some long range shots fired by another enemy aircraft, which broke away as soon as it realised its presence had been spotted.

McCudden turned for home, and despite the slight damage to B4981, he shot down another Rumpler over the lines on the way. This last machine would have

B489, in which McCudden brought down thirty-one enemy aircraft, fitted with the spinner from one of his victims, an LVG.

A8946 of 84 Squadron was shot down on 16 March 1918 by Lt Pinner of Jasta 13; its pilot, 2/Lt E. E. Dukes, was taken prisoner.

brought his score up to fifty, making him the first British pilot to achieve such a total, but his claim was disallowed due to a lack of witnesses. Understandably annoyed, McCudden promptly took off again, found yet another Rumpler and shot it down. In the evening, a British anti-aircraft battery telephoned to confirm his earlier claim, which was therefore allowed after all.

Major R. S. Dallas took over command of 40 Squadron in April 1918, making the conversion from the Sopwith Camels he had previously flown with one 15-minute flight in B4863. The Australian Dallas was originally an RNAS pilot, becoming part of the Royal Air Force on its formation on 1 April 1918. The German Spring Offensive led to the squadron flying low-level bombing and ground attack missions; on 14 April, Dallas was wounded in the leg and foot while attacking a convoy of trucks, flying B4879. He landed safely back at the squadron's base. Lost while flying a lone patrol on 1 June, he was credited with a total of ten victories while flying with 40 Squadron, bringing his official tally to thirty-nine, making him Australia's highest scoring pilot of the war.

Another 40 Squadron pilot, Capt. G. H. Lewis, was flying D3540 on 11 April when he spotted a formation of seven enemy aircraft and dived down to attack, only to find his guns had jammed. He broke off the action by diving away. With the jams cleared, he spotted a lone triplane and fired a long burst at it, sending it down in a slow spin; his victory claim was confirmed by an artillery battery. 40 Squadron's Capt. J. H. Tudhope also attacked a group of seven enemy aircraft the same day, sending one down with a burst from his Lewis gun.

At 84 Squadron, the South African pilot Anthony Beauchamp-Proctor scored his first victory – a two-seater sent down out of control on 3 January 1918 – while flying B539, a machine that had previously served with 60 Squadron until it was badly shot about in the dogfight that claimed the life of Werner Voss. At this time, the winter weather restricted the number of patrols flown and few enemy aircraft were seen, but over the next seven weeks, Beauchamp-Proctor achieved four more victories in B539, destroying an Albatros DV and sending a second Albatros, a Pfalz, and a Rumpler down out of control.

He then switched to D259, in which he scored four more, three of them – an Albatros DV and two Pfalz DIIIs – on 17 March 1918, bringing his total to nine. D259 was later flown by Lt R. Manser, who scored further victories in it before he himself was brought down on 18 June.

Meanwhile, Beauchamp-Proctor had been flying C1772, adding another ten to his score before its propeller was hit by a bursting anti-aircraft shell on 28 May; the resulting vibration damaged the airframe to such an extent that although it landed safely, it was considered not worth repairing. On 15 May, he took off at 3.25 a.m. and flew east, intending to catch the machines that had been bombing Amiens on their return home. At 3.55 a.m., he spotted a bomber coming back to land and attacked it, firing several hundred rounds, despite being under heavy fire from the ground. However, he not see it crash and could only claim it as damaged.

In June, Beauchamp-Proctor was posted back to the UK for a rest, returning to 84 Squadron in August and flying D6856, scoring a further nine victories before the machine was wrecked on 10 September. His final machine, which he took over that same day, was C1911, in which he also claimed nine victories before he was wounded by ground fire during a low-level mission on 8 October. C1911 was lost on 27 October. Its pilot, 2/Lt J. C. Collins, became a prisoner of war. Beauchamp-Proctor, his score standing at fifty-four, did not return to action and was killed in a flying accident while rehearsing for the 1921 Hendon Air Pageant.

Beauchamp-Proctor was acknowledged by his contemporaries as having the 'courage of a lion', a characteristic he displayed in his method of attacking the enemy. On 23 April, Mannock carefully picked off the rearmost machine from a formation of enemy Scouts and watched it crash. The same day saw Beauchamp-Proctor dive at the leader of another enemy formation, sending one down out of control in the ensuing dogfight. 23 April also saw Capt. C. C. Clark of 1 Squadron dive down on a group of eight Fokker triplanes in B8410, sending one of them down in flames.

60 Squadron suffered an unusual loss on 24 January when B4897 collided with an Albatros Scout from Jasta 7; both pilots were killed. On 19 February, 2/Lt Morley Kent, who hailed from Canada, shot down Albatros DVa with some remarkable marksmanship at a range of 400 yards. The German machine 4495/17 of Jasta 47 came down near Hollebeck on the Allied side of the lines, and its pilot

H7162, a rebuilt aircraft that joined 29 Squadron on 14 October 1918 and brought down at least five enemy aircraft was flown by 2/Lt E. G. Davies. Davies was killed when H7162's wings collapsed during a high-speed roll at Bickendorf on 6 February 1919.

Lt Von Puttkamen was taken as prisoner. Unfortunately, Kent was himself shot down just three days later.

In addition to losses in aerial combat, 60 Squadron suffered a number of casualties due to mechanical failure, one example occurring on 18 March when the engine of B545 failed. In the resulting forced landing, its pilot Capt. H. D. Crompton, was injured badly enough to require hospital treatment; his place as flight commander was taken by Capt. W. Copeland. On 9 June, the CC gear fitted to B8398 failed, stopping the engine and necessitating a forced landing in which the machine was wrecked and the pilot injured.

Ground forces also inflicted casualties to the squadron. For instance, Lt Cyril Ball, Albert Ball's younger brother who had only joined the squadron a few weeks before, was flying B533 on 5 February 1918 when a shell splinter hit his engine. As he tried to glide home, he was obliged to land hastily when attacked by a pilot from Jasta 26, becoming a prisoner of war. Lt Cambell's mount, D6182, was hit in the radiator by anti-aircraft fire on 23 June, but made a successful forced landing at Bertangles airfield. On 16 July, B186, flown by Lt R. Whitley, was hit by ground fire, damaging both the radiator and the fuselage frame, while on a trench-strafing mission. Lt J. Griffiths' D3503 was also hit, causing damage to the petrol tank, during the same mission.

On 17 May, Lt W. J. A. Duncan of 60 Squadron demonstrated exactly how Scout pilots might help reconnaissance machines to carry out their duties. When flying C9536, he spotted a lone R.E.8 being attacked by a group of German Albatroses and dived to its assistance, shooting down one of the enemy and keeping the rest engaged while the R.E.8 got away and made it safely back to its base.

McCudden, who following his investiture with the Victoria Cross at Buckingham Palace had been on leave in London, was keen to return to the front, and was given command of 60 Squadron. He flew out in a new S.E.5a, C1126, stopping on the way to visit his family who lived in Kent. After crossing the Channel, he stopped again at Auxi-le-Chateau in northern France to get directions to his new base. On taking off again, he hit the top of a tree and crashed, suffering injuries from which he died a few hours later.

India's only 'ace' pilot of the war was Indra Lal Roy. He flew with 56 Squadron for a few weeks in late 1917, but was injured when he crash landed his S.E.5a on 6 December. He returned to active duty in June 1918, and was posted to 40 Squadron. He shot down ten enemy aircraft in just two weeks, flying B180, beginning with a Hannover two-seater on 6 July. He brought down a DFW, several more Hannovers, a Pfalz, and three Fokker DVIIs, his last victory being yet another Hannover on 19 July. He was killed on 22 July while his patrol was in combat with a number of Fokker DVIIs.

On the morning of 10 August, Capt. H. J. Burden of 56 Squadron flew an offensive patrol in C1096, during which he attacked a group of enemy aircraft, sending down two, both of which were seen to crash. Later he attacked a second

S.E.5as of 29 Squadron lined up on 18 September 1918.

F8953, built by Vickers at Weybridge, joined 85 Squadron towards the end of the war.

No.1 Squadron's aircraft lined up, back to back, with the pilots and crews.

group, one of which broke up in the air, and on an evening patrol, he claimed two more victories. Two days later, he shot down three triplanes, with Capt. W. R. Irwin and Lt H. Molyneux each bringing one down in the same combat.

By the summer of 1918, the role of Scout pilots was changing, and although offensive patrols and aerial combat were still their main duty, ground attack missions became increasingly regular.

On 8 August, Lt N. W. R. Mawle of 64 Squadron, in D6917, attacked two German observation balloons that were being towed by teams of horses. Subjected to very heavy machine gun fire from the ground, he missed the first balloon, but managed to set the second on fire while at a height of just 25 feet. Although wounded in both his stomach and left arm, Mawle transferred his attention to an artillery battery, upsetting a limbered gun and scattering the horses.

4 October saw Lt R. A. Caldwell in B534 of 56 Squadron bring an observation balloon down in flames near Bohain-en-Vermandois, then turn back towards the lines at low level, attacking four limbered field guns, sending two into a ditch and scattering their mule teams. Next he fired at 150 yards range into a body of troops before turning his attention to further artillery batteries.

Four days later, Capt. Duncan Grinell-Milne, also of 56 Squadron, was attacking enemy artillery at low level when his machine, F5481, was hit by fragments from an anti-aircraft shell and descended rapidly, hitting the ground with sufficient force to wipe off the undercarriage. However, the ground had a slight downward slope at that point, and the S.E.5a, now missing its undercarriage, with half its tailplane broken off and trailing at the end of a bracing wire, and with a damaged propeller that made the engine vibrate badly, flew on just above the ground; it eventually crashed with such force that the engine was partly buried in the earth and the pilot knocked unconscious, but otherwise unhurt. Grinell-Milne was soon back in action in a replacement S.E.5a, C1149, and on 21 October, added a Fokker DVII to his score, diving down on it and firing about 150 rounds, then following it down to within a few hundred feet of the ground to watch it crash.

Other pilots continued to find aerial combat too, and on 30 October, a patrol from 74 Squadron met seven enemy aircraft, shooting five of them down with 2/Lt F. J. Hunt in C1137 claiming two, and Capt. A. C. Kiddle in F885, Lt W. C. Goudie in F5552, and Lt J. E. Ferrand claiming one each.

14

FOREIGN FIELDS AND OTHER FORCES

One S.E.5a, B4885, a 60 Squadron machine, underwent an unplanned change of nationality when it landed undamaged at Brielle in neutral Holland on 6 January 1918, just three days after joining the squadron after previous service with 56. Both it and its pilot, Lt Owen Thamer, were interned. The Dutch flew the machine to test and evaluate it, and then adopted it for use by their own air force, giving it the serial SE214, although of course, it took no further part in the war. After some negotiations, they formally purchased the machine from the British Government on 23 August 1918.

In addition to the fifteen squadrons on the Western Front, the S.E.5a flew and fought in the Middle East, with 72 Squadron in Mesopotamia, with 17, 47, and 150 Squadrons in Macedonia, and with 111 and 145 Squadrons in Palestine.

On 18 March 1918, B686, which joined 72 Squadron, then based at Samarra in what is now Iraq, achieved a spectacular victory on 21 April when Capt. J. S. Beatty attacked AEG two-seater 7065/17, firing just eight rounds from his Lewis gun before the enemy machine fell into a spin and crashed, both of its crew being killed. Beatty scored another victory flying B685, which joined 72 Squadron in April 1918, bringing down an Albatros DIII on 31 May. Lt H. Cannell used the same aircraft to force two unidentified enemy machines to land early in the morning of 27 June.

111 Squadron, which formed at Deir-el-Balah in Palestine in August 1917, added the S.E.5a B26 to its mixed collection of aircraft in October. This machine brought down an enemy two-seater on 19 February 1918, flown by Major Frederick W. Stent, the squadron's commanding officer at the time. The squadron acquired more S.E.5as at about this time, with B49 arriving on 4 February, B618 on 12 February, and B614 on 1 March. B617 followed a week later, with B616 joining the squadron on the day the Royal Air Force came into existence, 1 April 1918. Major Stent brought down several more enemy aircraft when flying B618, with Capt. Sutherland using it to send a two-seater down out of control on 30 May.

B692 with 47 Squadron in Macedonia. The camouflaged aeroplane behind it is an Armstrong Whitworth FK3.

As the Turkish opposition began to crumble, the RAF squadrons found themselves engaging in fewer aerial combats and more ground attack missions. When on 21 September 1918, the Turkish 7th Army was caught in the Wadi el Far'a area, attempting to cross the River Jordan, the S.E.5as of 111 and 145 Squadrons joined with aeroplanes from all the other squadrons in the area, including the DH9s of 144 Squadron and the F.E.2bs flown by No.1 Squadron AFC, in attacking the troops on the ground. Over 9 tons of bombs were dropped and more than 50,000 rounds of machine gun ammunition was fired, massacring the Turkish army and contributing to its final surrender the following month.

Altogether, a total of at least thirteen different S.E.5as served with 111 Squadron before it was disbanded after the war. 17 Squadron, which had formed at Gosport in February 1915, moved to Egypt later that year and to Salonika the following summer, operating a mixture of types, which from October 1917 included a number of S.E.5as. B613, a Vickers-built machine, arrived on 3 December 1917 and scored several victories, including an Albatros 'D' type Scout, which crashed into Lake Doiran on 31 March 1918. B28 joined the squadron on 14 December 1917, and flown by Capt. F. G. Saunders, brought down at least two enemy two-seaters before moving on to a new unit.

Formed as a home defence squadron at Beverley in March 1916, equipped with B.E.2cs and F.K.3s, 47 Squadron was sent out to Macedonia in September 1916, still operating a mixture of two-seaters. Early in 1918, it began to re-equip with the S.E.5a, receiving B689 on 23 January, B688 on 3 February, and at least five

B139 served in Palestine and is seen here fitted with bombs ready for a ground attack mission.

more aircraft from the same production batch over the next few weeks. One of these, B695, was credited with the destruction of six enemy aircraft while flown by Lt C. B. Green, and another when Lt J. A. Beeney took it over.

On 1 April, both 17 and 47 Squadrons were re-designated as corps squadrons, retaining their two-seaters, but their fighter flights, and thus their S.E.5as, were transferred to 150 Squadron, which was formed exclusively as a fighter unit, operating Sopwith Camels and Bristol Monoplanes, as well as the S.E.5a. New machines assigned to the squadron included C9501, which arrived on 3 July, and D3495, which joined the squadron a month later, and in which Capt. G. G. Bell scored at least four victories.

Pilots from the British Empire formed a large proportion of the Royal Flying Corps, coming from Canada, South Africa, and even India, and serving as part of regular squadrons. However, the Australians, in keeping with their emerging national character, preferred to operate in units that were, as far as possible, wholly Australian. Thus, 68 Squadron RFC, which was formed in Egypt with Australian personnel during 1916, never regarded itself as anything but No. 2 Squadron Australian Flying Corps, a title that was eventually officially recognised in January 1918. The squadron moved to England in January 1917 for training, and served in France flying the DH5 until these were replaced with S.E.5as, the conversion beginning in December 1917. The Australian pilots often operated in pairs, and on 18 February Lt Huxley and Lt Paxton made the first contact with the enemy when they encountered four Albatros Scouts, which they engaged, Huxley sending one down out of control.

S.E.5as of No. 6 Training Squadron, Australian Flying Corps, Minchinhampton, with a line of Avro 504ks in the background.

On 22 March, as the German army made its big push forward, the skies were filled with enemy aircraft, and Lt H. G. Forrest, flying C9539, brought down three – a two-seater and two Scouts. Lt McKenzie, in C5382, sent an Albatros down out of control, C9641 sent another Albatros into a spin, and Lt Holden downed yet another; a total of six victories in a single patrol.

With No. 2 Squadron AFC was Lt Frank Alberry from Tasmania, who had lost a leg after being shot in the knee while serving in the trenches, but had become a pilot despite his disability. He joined the squadron in June 1918, and scored a total of seven combat victories flying S.E.5as, including D1696, D6948, and D6995, the first two being written off in forced landings following engine failure.

On 7 July, while the squadron was flying a ground attack mission, the Squadron CO Major Murray James, bombed the railway at Harbourdin from a height of just 50 feet, two of his bombs straddling a locomotive. This kind of mission was common as the Allies began to push forward, although both offensive patrols and escort duties remained the squadron's daily routine.

The Australians also operated their own training squadron, based at Aston Down, near Minchinhampton in Gloucestershire, whose equipment included the S.E.5a.

When the USA entered the war in April 1917, it initiated what was intended to be the biggest aircraft building programme the world had ever seen. A commission was sent to Europe, visiting England, France, and Italy, to select suitable designs

C9539 of 2 Squadron AFC at Savvy in March 1918. It scored a number of victories flown by Capt. H. G. Forrest until it was declared unfit for further service and struck off charge on 8 July 1918.

An officer of 2 Squadron AFC stands proudly by B27, apparently oblivious of the activities of the mechanic working on the engine.

Two S.E.5as of 'A' flight, 2 Squadron AFC, in November 1918.

Another view of C8747, providing shelter from the sun for some well-dressed American soldiers.

for mass production; one of those selected was the S.E.5a, not as a fighter, for the Americans were already looking for the next generation of combat designs, but as an advanced trainer. Licences were negotiated and drawings obtained. Several examples, including B503, C1115, and C1119-1121, were purchased by the commission and shipped to the USA, arriving in July 1918, largely as samples to aid manufacture.

Inevitably, all this took time, and it was not until April 1918 that the choice between the S.E.5a and the SPAD was finally settled in favour of the former, the

D343, one of a batch shipped to America for evaluation, apparently being assembled after arrival.

deciding factor being that the S.E.5a was rather easier to fly. An order was placed on 8 June 1918, with the Curtiss Aeroplane and Motor Company, for 1,000 machines, to be powered by 180-hp direct-drive derivatives of the Hispano-Suiza engine built by Wright-Martin. Only one machine, serial SC43153, was built; it was tested and submitted for official trials by 20 August 1918. Initially, the engine overheated badly; a defect finally cured by an increase in radiator area, which was achieved by adding a third core in the upper part of the space between the two Viper-style blocks. The machine was eventually accepted, but Armistice came before any more could be completed and the order was cancelled.

While awaiting receipt of the results of the mass production programme, the US Army Air Service purchased sufficient aeroplanes from European manufacturers to get its squadrons into action; these included over 100 S.E.5as, including C8738-8757, C9073-90, and D6101-1112. These machines were all bought new, but D6096, which had previously served with 56 Squadron RFC and had brought down at least one enemy aircraft, an Albatros, became American property too.

F8001-8200, from a batch of 250 built by Austin, were also sold to the US Army Air Service, some of them equipping the 25th and 141th Aero squadrons, and the remainder being shipped to the USA. The 141st Squadron commenced operations in October 1918, but the 25th did not get its first S.E.5a until 1 November, and

Two Austin-built S.E.5as after shipping to the USA. As was common, no Lewis gun is fitted and the upper engine cowling has been removed.

Two S.E.5as from the batch built by Austin in the USA. They have Viper engines and the original steel tube undercarriage.

C8747, another machine that was shipped to the USA. The upper engine cowling, Lewis gun, and Aldis sights are all missing.

F8006 heads a line-up of the US Army's 25 Aero Squadron.

flew just two patrols before the Armistice, with no enemy aircraft seen on either occasion. Machines known to have served with the squadron include F8005, F8006, F8010, F8015, and F8030, the latter bearing the name *Virginia*.

These machines retained their original serial numbers while in France, but new identities, often based on their original serial, were given to those shipped to the States, as with F8148 for example, which went to Selfridge Field, Michigan, becoming AS8148.

15

AFTER THE WAR

At the time of the Armistice, around 2,900 S.E.5/5as had been delivered, but it was some time before contracts were cancelled; a total of 5,265 were eventually manufactured, the last example being delivered in April 1919.

The run down of the huge RAF contingent in France and other war zones commenced early in 1919, with squadrons disbanded and their aircraft and equipment disposed of. The S.E.5as were spared the indignity of being 'reduced to produce' in situ, which was the fate of many other machines, including Sopwith Camels, and were shipped back to England. Machines from numbers 24, 40, 56, and 94 Squadrons, the latter having only arrived in France in November 1918, were taken to 1 Squadron's aerodrome at Le Hameau, and those from 41, 60, 64, 74, and 85 joined 32 Squadron at Serny for ferrying onward to England.

By the middle of 1919, only 29, 84, and 92 Squadrons were still equipped with S.E.5as, forming part of the Army of Occupation in Germany. 92 Squadron was disbanded in Germany in August 1919; the other two squadrons returned home at the same time and were disbanded at the end of the year. The last RAF squadron to receive the S.E.5a was 81, which having disbanded in July 1918 when equipped with Sopwith 'Dolphins', reformed two days after the Armistice with largely Canadian personnel. It received S.E.5as, including E5755, in March 1919, operating them until it was disbanded in February 1920, thus ending the S.E.5a's career in front-line service with the Royal Air Force.

As we have already seen, development continued after the Armistice, with S.E.5as being used, especially at Farnborough, for a number of experiments. Some were intended to improve the machine's own performance, such as a scheme devised during 1919 for the fitting of a Sutton Harness, including shoulder straps in place of the single broad seatbelt usually used. Other experiments were of a more general nature. For example, E5927, which had already being the subject of various experiments, was used by Capt. G. H. Norman, then head of the Engine Research Department of the Royal Aircraft Establishment for experiments with on-board fire extinguishers. During the development of fire extinguishers, E5927

F934 of 29 Squadron, which arrived in France about a week after the Armistice.

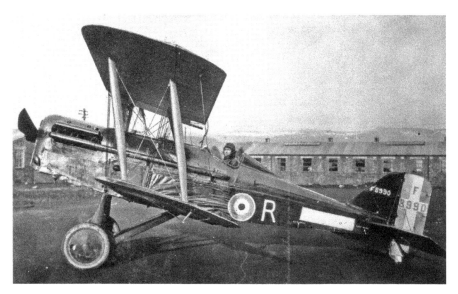

F8990 with 74 Squadron after the war.

was frequently set alight, and the plywood decking had to be renewed several times in order to test the effectiveness of the extinguisher. By the summer of 1921, Norman had sufficient confidence in it to deliberately set light to his machine while flying. The fire was put out without problem, but Norman crashed attempting to land, his eyesight still badly affected by the smoke. He died a few weeks later in Cambridge Military Hospital, Aldershot, possibly as a result.

D7020 at the Royal Aircraft Establishment after the war. It remained there until 1926 and later joined the civil register as G-EBQM.

E5927 was evidently repaired, or rebuilt, as a machine with that serial was later used in tests of what was described as both an 'exhaust muff cockpit heater' and a thermostatic radiator shutter control. On 12 July 1924, it force landed during a speed test and was again repaired, being reported as extant, at Farnborough, as late as 1926. In a continuing investigation into stability and manoeuvrability, D600 was rigged without dihedral and filmed in flight, the camera operator being in the rear cockpit of a Bristol Fighter flying alongside, with D7022, rigged as standard, being filmed for comparison.

As aeroplane performance increased, it became increasingly obvious that the selection of a propeller for any machine was a compromise. When taking off, the propeller needs to apply the engine's maximum power while the aeroplane, and therefore the airstream over it, is moving relatively slowly; at level flight, it needs to apply this power when the airstream is moving much more quickly. Climbing presents yet another, slightly different requirement. The solution was to design a propeller in which the pitch, that is the angle at which the blades meet the air, could be altered in flight. Testing of the Hart variable pitch propeller, comprising wooden blades fitted into an aluminium hub, had begun using S.E.5a C1134 in October 1918, but proved unsuccessful, for the blades could not be properly secured in their sockets, as the pitch changed as it spun. There is no record of a flight being attempted. A second, improved version, designed by the RAE, was tested on C1148 in the spring of 1919, and later on C1091, with development and testing continuing at least until April 1920. Although ultimately successful, the device was considered an unnecessary complication, and the fixed-pitch wooden propeller would remain standard for almost another twenty years before advances in performance forced the change.

A variable-pitch propeller, designed by the RAE fitted to C1091. The long rod along the fuselage side is part of the operating mechanism.

A new type of tailskid was designed and patented by Capt. John Palethorpe; a hydraulic damper absorbed the landing shocks and maintained contact with the ground while a helical spring was employed for taxiing. It was tested during 1919 on both D7007 and D7012, the latter machine suffering an accident during the trials.

Testing of parachutes, which had begun during the war and which had yet to reach a conclusion, continued both at Martlesham Heath and Farnborough. Both the Calthrop Guardian Angel A.1 and that designed by Capt. F. C. Mears were tested, with S.E.5as E5696 and F5278 being modified to accommodate them. The Guardian Angel was a static line design in which the container is fixed to the aeroplane, and the canopy is released as the user falls by a cord that pulls it from the container. The aeroplane's rear fuselage was modified to provide the necessary accommodation, while the Mears was a backpack type, requiring a modified seat. Neither type was adopted.

A8947, the former S.E.5b, was flown in the 1920 RAF pageant by Squadron Leader Jack Noakes, who put on an impressive display of aerobatics, enhancing his growing reputation as the master of the art. It was damaged on 27 January 1921 when it suffered engine failure while flying near Guildford. The machine collided with a hedge in a forced landing and appears not to have been repaired.

E5696 at the RAE after the war, apparently being started up as the pilot's hand is on the starting magneto. The rear fuselage has been modified to accommodate a parachute.

Also in January 1921, R. M. Hill began a series of experiments at the request of the Accidents Investigation Committee into the lateral stability of the S.E.5a with the rudder inoperative. D7020 and 7022 were each tested, both when gliding and with the engine throttled for level flight, turns being made on the ailerons alone. When gliding, the propeller stopped, but then turned in a series of jerks, pausing as each piston was on its compression stroke and then moving on with a jolt that could be felt in the cockpit. The report of the trials, BA382, published on 14 March 1921, concluded that although stable when gliding with the engine on, the machine would turn left without use of the rudder, but when turning right, the nose dropped and the machine entered a steepening spiral.

At the 1923 RAF Pageant, as its annual flying displays were then called, five S.E.5as from the RAE performed formation aerobatics, their pilots being Flt Lt P. W. S. Bulman, Flt Lt E. R. Scholefield, and Flt Lt G. S. Oddie, Flg Off. J. Chick and Flg Off. H. Junor.

Other S.E.5as employed as test vehicles at the RAE Farnborough included C1069, which suffered a forced landing on Laffan's Plain on 17 March 1920, D314, and D7016-7023. Although D7021 crashed on 27 August 1920, the remainder of the batch stayed in service until about the middle of the decade, three of them joining the civil register, with D7016 becoming G-EBPA, D7020 becoming G-EBQA, and D7022, which has already been mentioned in connection with stability trials, becoming G-EPBD.

In order to facilitate the building up of their air services, Britain made a gift of aeroplanes to a number of her Dominions, together with spare engines, motor transport, and even hangars. Among the aeroplanes thus donated were twelve S.E.5as to Canada, twenty-two to South Africa, and thirty-five to Australia.

Five S.E.5as that performed aerobatics at the 1923 RAF Aerial Pageant.

Those shipped to Australia included D8431, D8471, and E3169-3171, arriving at Melbourne in 1921, although none were assembled immediately upon arrival, and were left crated until sufficient squadrons had been formed to operate them. Some were never assembled, although the serial numbers A2-1 to A2-35 were assigned to the whole batch.

Five S.E.5as from Point Cook flew north, intending to take part in a flypast at the official opening of Canberra as the nation's capital on 9 May 1927, but one ground looped at Cootamundra and three other suffered damage in one way or another; reserve machines from Richmond had to be used instead. One machine, A2-24, left the formation due to an unknown cause, and crashed about half a mile from the Government building. The pilot, Flg Off. F. Ewen, sustained injuries from which he died later the same day.

The following day, the surviving Point Cook machine, A2-11, suffered a drop in oil pressure on its journey home with photographs of the opening ceremony. It came down in some trees when its engine seized, and was wrecked. The pilot, Sgt Orme Denny, was knocked temporarily unconscious, but was otherwise unharmed and was able to make the long walk to find assistance. The wrecked machine was eventually located, not without difficulty, and the photographs were recovered; the remainder of the machine was left in situ where it was to remain undisturbed for over thirty-five years.

At least one machine, A2-16, was fitted with an oleo undercarriage. Australia also acquired a two-seat trainer, which was given the serial A2-36, and had two

Australia's A2-13 appears to be as originally manufactured, except for the removal of the Lewis gun and Foster Mounting.

over-wing petrol tanks, similar to those originally fitted to the early S.E.5s. It survived until 24 October 1928 when a DH9a taxied into it, causing extensive damage.

Of Australia's thirty-five single-seat S.E.5as, ten were scrapped following crashes, including A2-13 (ex-D8476), which crashed at Point Cook on 1 March 1926, and A2-19 (ex-D8490), which crashed on 22 February 1927, killing its pilot, Cadet A. Dix. At least eleven were never assembled, and the remainder were finally replaced by Bristol Bulldogs in 1930. South Africa's twenty-two S.E.5as, like all Imperial Gift machines, were Viper powered, including D8478, D8483, D8493-8494, D8500, E3167, F7773-7779, and F7781-7785.

E3167 made its first flight in South Africa on 21 September 1919, but its new owners then decided to use only the DH4 and DH9 two-seaters, which had also formed part of the Imperial Gift, for operations; almost all of the rest of the S.E.5as remained crated until 1926, when wastage among the others types forced their use. They then remained in service until 1929. E3167 became 301, D8500 became 302, F7783 became 303, and F7774 became 312, although it would appear that these new identities were never marked on the machines; indeed, they may not have been allocated until they were struck off charge as a kind of retrospective effort to update their records.

Those sent to Canada, arriving in 1920, were all given civilian registrations, with for example, D8472 becoming G-CYBI, E3172 becoming G-CYAB, and F9139 becoming G-CYCV. Almost all served at Camp Borden in Ontario, the birthplace

309, one of the South African Air Force's Imperial Gift S.E.5as.

and premier training station of the RCAF, and at least one, G-CYCE (ex-F9177), appears to have been converted to have two cockpits and dual controls. Wastage due to accidents slowly reduced their numbers, with G-CYBX (ex-D8489) being written off as early as January 1921, and G-CYBQ being written off in March of the following year. At least five more were struck off charge at the end of April 1926, the reminder surviving until 1929.

Early in 1919, a dispute arose between Poland and the post-revolutionary Soviet Russia, which quickly escalated into an armed conflict. The air services of both Poland and the anti-Bolshevik, or White Russian, area of Belarus each acquired a number of S.E.5as, with one of the Polish machines being captured intact after a forced landing. It was then operated by the Bolshevik forces, and painted with the red star markings of Soviet Russia. The twenty-four White Russian machines included B8305, B8309, C6374-6381, D3544, and D3550-3552.

Another nation whose air services included the S.E.5a was Argentina, whose solitary example AC-21 survived until at least January 1929 when it crashed on landing, damaging the undercarriage. Elsewhere in South America, the Chilean air service had a total of eight S.E.5as: C9182-9184, C9204, E5814, E5958-5959, and E5962.

Another solitary S.E.5a, powered by a Viper engine, found its way to Japan along with the official trade mission headed by the allegedly traitorous Master of Sempill, and was operated by the Imperial Japanese Navy.

After the war, the USAAS shipped home the remaining S.E.5as that had equipped its squadrons in France, to join other examples that had been shipped to the States while the conflict was in progress. These served, as intended by the purchasing

Argentina's only S.E.5a, AC-21, following a crash landing at Sarmiento on 24 January 1929.

Col. H. Hickham stands proudly in front of an S.E.5a at Bolling Field, near Washington DC, USA, in May 1920.

An unidentified S.E.5a in postwar US service. The original broad seat belt has been replaced with a full harness, including shoulder straps. The building in the background appears to be still under construction.

This S.E.5a in the USA during the 1920s has had the headrest fairing, Lewis gun, and foster mounting removed, although the Vickers gun appears to be still in place.

An Eberhart rebuilt machine, in US markings, in flight. As was common, the upper engine cowling has been removed, although whether this was done to facilitate maintenance or to improve cooling is unclear.

commission, as advanced trainers, the majority being based at Kelly Field, near San Antonio in Texas.

During 1922-23, fifty machines were rebuilt by the Eberhart Steel Products Corporation with ply-covered fuselages and 180-hp Wright-Martin engines. They were given the serial numbers A.S. 22-276 to A.S. 22-325 and were re-designated the S.E.5E to distinguish them from the originals that had been shipped from England. The type remained in service as an advanced trainer until 1927.

Two S.E.5as, D6106 and D6111, also served with the US Navy as A-5888 and A-5889, one being mounted on a turret platform aboard the USS *Mississippi*.

16

CIVILIAN LIFE

On 16 July 1921, the universities of Oxford and Cambridge moved their traditional rivalry from the river into the air in what was termed 'The Aerial Boat Race'. The event appears to have been suggested by A. R. Boeree, a former Martlesham Heath test pilot then reading for a degree at Oriel College, Oxford, and was supported by the Royal Aero Club, which provided the aircraft. A batch of eight Martinsyde-built S.E.5as were hired for the occasion from the Aircraft Disposal Company and registered G-EAXQ-EAXX; six were to race and two were spares. Since the universities were full of ex-RFC/RAF pilots, who like Boeree had returned to complete their education, there was no shortage of applications to take part. The teams finally selected were: Oxford: A. R. Boeree (Oriel), N. Pring (New), and A. V. Hurley (Keeble); Cambridge: A. Francis (Caius), W. S. Philcox (Caius), and R. K. Muir (St Catherine's).

Held on the same day as the Aerial Derby, the 129-mile course comprised three laps of a circuit from the start at Hendon via Epping and Hertford. To aid identification and encourage spectator support, the tails of the S.E.5as were painted in the university colours of dark blue for Oxford and light blue for Cambridge.

The Cambridge team flew the course high, hoping for better engine performance in the cooler air, while the Oxford pilots stayed low. The Cambridge tactic proved the move effective, as Philcox in G-EAXU (ex-F5333) crossed the line first at the end of each of the three laps. On the final lap, an ignition lead broke on Pring's mount G-EAXW (ex-F5259) and he force landed in a field near Enfield. The other machines all completed the course with little more than seconds between then; the final result was a victory for Cambridge, whose team took the first three places, with Boeree, whose idea it had been, finishing last. Although considered a success, the race was not held again.

G-EAXQ (ex-F5249) was entered in the 1922 Aerial Derby, flown by the Aircraft Disposal Company's test pilot Herbert Perry, but failed to complete the race and was scrapped. G-EAXU crashed at Croydon the following April and was written off. G-EAXT (ex-F5258) and G-EAXW were scrapped in November 1922. The

G-EAXW, formerly F5259, was flown by N. Pring of New College, Oxford, in the 'Aerial Boat Race' of 1921, but failed to complete the course.

certificates of airworthiness of the remaining racers were not renewed, and it is probable that they too were scrapped, the parts being sold for whatever price they would fetch. This practice was the principal business of the Aircraft Disposal Company, although it continued to offer S.E.5as for sale, complete but unarmed, for £700, albeit with few takers.

In addition to the eight machines hired for the aerial boat race, at least ten other S.E.5as appeared on the civil register in the hands of private owners. These included E6013, which was completed too late for military service, and which as G-EAZT became the property of Dr E. R. Whitehead Reid of Canterbury, a well-known private flying enthusiast in the 1920s; he claimed, probably for the benefit of the tax inspectors, that he used it to visit distant patients. It was fitted with a 90-hp RAF1a engine, an air-cooled V8, which must have reduced fuel consumption (as well as performance), and simplified maintenance. However, it nosed over while taxiing at Bekesbourne early in 1923, and was not repaired. Instead, Dr Whitehead Reid acquired G-EBCA (ex-E5956), fitted with an 80-hp Renault, another air-cooled V8, reducing its maximum speed to about 65 mph, which he entered in the Grosvenor Trophy Race at Lympne on 23 June 1923. He continued to fly the aircraft for some years, and it remained on the civil register until 1930.

Other machines fitted with less powerful engines included G-EBTK, which had a 90-hp RAF1a, and which was owned at one time by Mr L. R. Oldmeadows, and G-EBTQ, to which was fitted a 120-hp 'Airdisco' engine, developed by the Aircraft Disposal Company from the 80-hp Renault. G-EBTQ was acquired by the music hall, and later by film star Will Hay in 1927, but the registration was cancelled in 1930.

G- EBCA, formerly F5956, with a neatly installed 80-hp Renault engine, at Bekesbourne, while owned by R. Wigglesworth.

G-EBCA with a rather more angular cowling later in its civil career.

G-EBPA, ex-D7016, with shortened exhaust pipes. The pilot appears to be seated unusually high, as in the original design.

Dudley Watts' racing S.E.5a, designated DW1. The rear fuselage has been modified to improve streamlining and it was reported to have been fitted with a 300-hp Hispano-Suiza engine.

Allen Wheeler, then a fairly recently qualified RAF pilot, bought S.E.5a G-EBQM (ex-D7020) in March 1927, allegedly for just £25, and later that year, entered it in the Aerial Derby. G-EBPA and G-EBOG were also entered, the latter being the property of Dudley Watt, later modified by Watt to become the DW1 racer, fitted with a 300-hp Hispano-suiza engine.

Another serving RAF pilot with a privately owned S.E.5a was Flg Off. H. R. D. Waghorn, who kept it at Wittering during 1926/27.

A further thirty-two surplus S.E.5as were all registered over time to one man, Major John Clifford Savage. 'Jack' Savage had been manager to the racing and exhibition pilot B. C. Hucks in the years before the war, and watching Hucks perform aerobatics, wondered if there was some way in which the aircraft's path through the air might be made visible. It was an idea that stayed with him, and by 1920, he had patented a method of doing just that by adding an oil-based chemical to the engine exhaust to produce a huge volume of dense, pale grey smoke. His idea was now to write advertising slogans in the sky. Savage bought Vickers-built S.E.5a F9022, now registered as G-EATE, from the Aircraft Disposal Company at Croydon in February 1922, and modified it to produce the smoke at his base at Hendon. The tank for the oil was fitted into the fuselage, and the exhaust pipes were extended to join aft of the tail – the rudder being bifurcated to accommodate them – and were wrapped in asbestos rope to keep the gases

Something of an enigma; this S.E.5a carries a British civil registration G-EBGL, but bears the legend 'The Skywriting Corporation of America'. Although it has a modified nose and underslung radiator, it has not been modified to produce smoke. It was originally built by Austin Motors, construction number 1662, as F7960.

Another Savage Skywriter, G-EBVB, seen in 1933. It had previously been shipped to Australia in 1928, returning later the same year.

Savage's S.E.5a, in Germany around 1932.

G-EBIB while in service as a Savage Skywriter. It is now on display in the London Science Museum.

Savage Skywriter G-EBIC during its working life. It is now displayed in the RAF Museum, restored to its original serial, F938.

hot. The converted machine was test flown by Cyril Turner. An initial problem of starting and stopping the smoke precisely when required was eventually solved, the method becoming the subject of another patent.

Savage also worked out how best to form the letters, writing upside down so that the message could be read from below, with the machine following a flat course, turning without banking, at a height of around 10,000 feet.

By 1922, all was ready and Turner wrote the word 'VIM' (a well known brand of scouring powder) in the sky, with Savage using photographs of the message to sell the idea to potential advertisers. Uptake was immediate, and on 30 May 1922, the word 'CASTROL' appeared over Epsom Downs on derby day, with a 6-mile-long 'DAILY MAIL' written over London a few days later for millions to see, before being repeated around the country. 'PERSIL' also appeared, as did 'VIM' – now being paid for – and the Savage Skywriting Company expanded rapidly, acquiring more and more S.E.5as for conversion at Hendon, where the company was based.

France and Belgium were soon included in Savage's operations, and in November 1922, he shipped a converted S.E.5a to the USA aboard the Cunard liner *Mauretania*, announcing its arrival with the words 'Hello USA' in the sky above New York, following it the next day with his telephone number. A total of nine S.E.5as were shipped to the USA, where a separate company, The Skywriting Corporation of America, owned by Savage, was formed to operate them; its activities continued until 1927 when the aeroplanes were sold off.

Operations in England continued a little longer, but as skywriting lost its impact, orders slowed and the company Skywriting Ltd was wound up in the early 1930s, although a few of its aeroplanes, including G-EBDT, G-EBIF, G-EBXC, G-EBXL, and G-EBTM, went to join the company in Germany, continuing skywriting there until 1935.

The majority of the Savage skywriting machines were scrapped, although two, G-EBIA and G-EBIC, were sold, the latter to Mr R. G. Nash in 1937. G-EBIB was presented by Savage to the Science Museum at South Kensington in London.

17

THE S.E.5 TODAY

A total of six complete original examples have survived and are preserved in museums around the world. A number of full-scale reproductions also exist, some including original components, some built to fly, and others as museum exhibits. There also exist a large number of scale reproductions built for sport flying, which although differing considerably from the original construction, give some sense of what the S.E.5a was like to fly.

The original examples include three ex-Savage skywriters, G-EBIA, EBIB, and EBIC, which are displayed in UK museums. G-EBIA forms part of the Shuttleworth Collection of Historic Aeroplanes based at Old Warden Aerodrome in Bedfordshire, where it still occasionally performs in flying displays and is now painted with what is believed to be its original identity, F904. One pilot who flew it recorded that it accelerates to take off with very little swing, the rudder being effective almost immediately, and after a small forward stick movement at about 30 mph to raise the tail, lifts off and climbs at 60 mph. Control forces are light to moderate, the ailerons create a lot of adverse drag and lots of rudder input is needed to overcome this. Directional stability is adequate and longitudinal stability very good, and it handles very well apart from a rather slow rate of roll. It lands at 50 mph with the engine idling at 1,100 rpm, the landing roll being about 200 yards in calm air, reducing to 100 yards with a 10-knot wind.

G-EBIC is on display at the Royal Air Force Museum at Hendon, London, painted in original markings as F938. The last of the trio, G-EBIB, hangs in the aeronautical gallery of the Science Museum in London's South Kensington, and after a period on display in RFC markings, it has been returned to the modified appearance it had when Mr Jack Savage handed it over at the end of its skywriting career.

The Australian War Memorial Museum in Canberra displays the last survivor of the country's Imperial Gift machines, A2-4 (ex-C1916), while at the Ditsong Museum of Military History in Saxonwold, Transvaal, South Africa, the last of that nation's S.E.5as, F7781/3, is also on display.

The Shuttleworth Collection's F904 in flight.

The Science Museum's G-EBIB displayed as a Savage Skywriter.

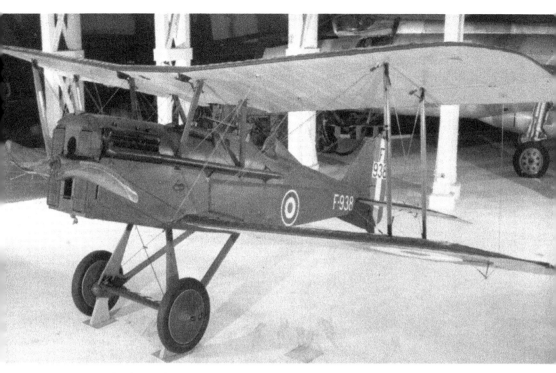

F938 on display at the RAF Museum in Hendon.

South Africa's F7781/3 when it was on display in Johannesburg.

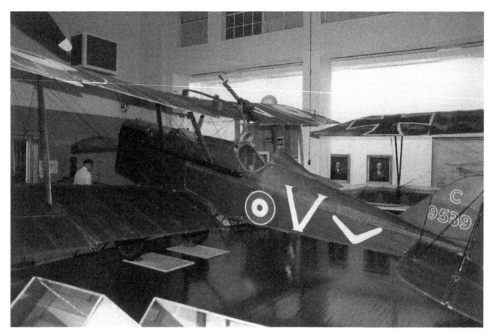

A2-4 on display at the Australian War Memorial in Canberra. It is marked as C9539, an aircraft of 2 Squadron AFC, which scored numerous victories flown by, among others, Capt. H. G. Forrest.

Two reproduction S.E.5as in flight over their home base in New Zealand. A third example was constructed at the same time and the three frequently fly together in displays.

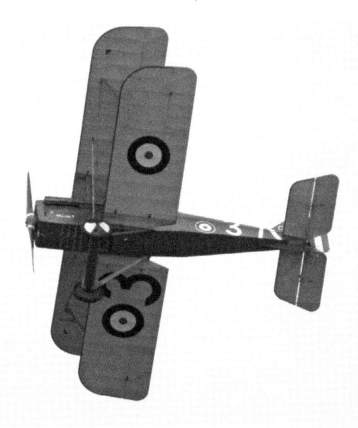

A reproduction S.E.5a in flight during a flying display at its home base of La Ferte Alais near Paris.

A typical example of the many scale reproduction S.E.5as owned and flown by home-builders the world over. This one is from Arizona in 2007. In comparison to full-scale machines, the nose is shallow and the vertical tail surfaces are overly large.

A scale reproduction S.E.5a powered by a Rolls Royce 'Continental' engine, owned by Mike Speakman, and based at North Coates airfield in Lincolnshire. The original F5459 was, at one time, rigged with reduced dihedral. It achieved at least one victory, downing a Fokker DVII.

The United States Air Force Museum at Dayton, Ohio, houses the only surviving Eberhart-rebuilt S.E.5E, AS22-325, which began life as B8525, built by Austin Motors.

The numerous, full-scale reproductions displayed in various museums around the world include F5475 at the Brooklands Museum in Surrey, where so many examples were originally built, and F943 at the Yorkshire Air Museum at Elvington. The Australian Air Force Museum at Point Cook also has a superb reproduction S.E.5a, as do a number of museums in North America.

The Memorial Flight at La Ferte Alais, near Paris, operates flying example A8898 (F-AZCY), which incorporates some original components, including the petrol tank, while the Vintage Aviator Collection, based at Hood Aerodrome, Masterton, New Zealand, includes a flight of three reproductions, all perfectly accurate, which perform regularly together in public displays.

There are many other examples, too many to list, around the world, some accurate reproductions built closely to the original drawings, and others merely representative of the type, and not intended for close examination. In addition to these full-size examples, there are a great many scale facsimiles, around 85 per cent full size – many home-built – that allow the private pilot to enjoy something of the pleasure of flying this great First World War fighter, and so help keep its memory alive.

18

DATA SCHEDULE

	S.E.5	S.E.5a	S.E.5b	S.E.5E
Engine	150-hp Hispano-Suiza	200-hp Wolseley Viper	200-hp Hispano-Suiza	180-hp Wright
Propeller	T.28041	AB662	---	---
Span-upper	28'-0"	26'-7"	30'-7"	26'-7"
Span-lower	28'-0"	26'-7"	26'-6"	26'-7"
Chord-upper	5'-0"	5'-0"	6'-0"	5'-0"
Chord-lower	5'-0"	5'-0"	4'-3"	5'-0"
Gap	4'-7"	4'-7"	4'-7"	4'-7"
Wing area (square feet)	249.8	245.8	278	245.8
Stagger	1'-6"	1'-6"	---	1'-6"
Length	20'-11"	20'-11"	20'-10"	20'-11"
Height	9'-6"	9'-6"	9'-6"	20'-11"
Empty weight (lb)	1,280	1,406	---	---
Loaded weight (lb)	1,850	1,950	1,950	2,060
Speed (mph) (sea level)	128	134	---	129
Speed (mph) (10,000 feet)	114	126	---	117
Ceiling (feet)	18,000	22,000	---	---
Climb to 10,000 feet	14 min. 15 seconds	10 min. 50 seconds	---	13 min.

PRODUCTION BATCHES

Royal Aircraft Factory, Farnborough, Hampshire:
A4561-4563; A4845-4868; A8898-8947; B4851-4900; C1051-C1150; D7001-7050 (cancelled from D7025).

Air Navigation Company Ltd, Addlestone, Surrey (formerly Bleriot & SPAD):
C1751-1950; E5937-6036; H634-733 (cancelled from H711).

Austin Motor Company Ltd, Birmingham:
B8231-8580; C8861-9310; E5837-5936; F7951-8200; H5291-5500 (cancelled).

Martinsyde Ltd, Brooklands, Surrey:
B1-200; D3911-4011; E3154-3253; F5248-5348; F8321-8420 (cancelled).

Vickers Ltd (Aviation Department), Crayford, Kent:
C5301-5450; D301-450; D8431-8580; E1251-1400; E3154-3253; F551-615.

Vickers Ltd (Aviation Department), Weybridge, Surrey:
B501-700; C9486-9635; D201-300; D3426-3575; E3904-4103; F5449-5698; F8946-9145.

Whitehead Aircraft Ltd, Richmond, Surrey:
B1001-1100 (cancelled).

Wolseley Motors Ltd, Birmingham:
C6351-6580; D6851-7000; F851-950; F7751-7800 (cancelled from F7782).

Rebuilds:
B733; B848; B875; B891; B8436; B7733; B7735; B7737; B7765; B7770-7771; B7786-7787; B7798; B7824; B7830-7833; B7850; B7870; B7881; B7890-7891; B7899; B7901; B8791; B8932; F4176; F4575; F5910; F5912; F5924; F5956; F6276; F6427; F6431-6432; F9568; H7072-7074; H7161-7166; H7181; H7247-7254; H7256-7261.

19

S.E.5 ACES

The following list includes all those pilots identified as having claimed ten or more victories flying the S.E.5/5a.

Also included, out of respect, is Albert Ball whose practical suggestions and modifications helped make the S.E.5 the success it was.

Name	Score in S.E.5	Total Score
A. F. Beauchamp-Proctor	54	54
J. T. B. McCudden	51	57
G. E. H. McElroy	47	47
E. C. Mannock	45	61
W. G. Claxton	37	37
J. I. T. Jones	37	37
W. A. Bishop	36	72
F. R. G. McCall	32	35
G. H. Bowman	30	32
P. J. Clayson	29	29
R. T. C Hoidge	28	28
G. J. C. Maxwell	26	26
A. P. F. Rhys-Davids	25	25
F. O. Soden	25	27
W. E. Shields	24	24
T. F. Hazell	23	43
B. Roxburgh-Smith	22	22
T. S. Harrison	22	22
J. A. Slater	21	24

Name	Score in S.E.5	Total Score
L. M. Barlow	20	20
C. H. R. Lagesse	20	20
R. A. Maybery	20	20
C. G. Ross	20	20
W. A. Southey	20	20
H. D. Barton	19	19
H. A. Kullberg	19	19
A. E. Reed	19	19
W. C. Lambert	18	18
C. F. Falkenberg	17	17
K. L. Caldwell	17	25
A. K. Cowper	17	25
I. D. R. McDonald	17	20
G. J. Rose	16	16
F. R. Smith	16	16
E. R. Tempest	16	17
H. J. Burden	16	16
R. A. Grosvenor	16	16
C. J. Venter	16	16
C. M. Crowe	15	19
H. B. Richardson	15	15
H. A. Saunders	15	15
A. C. Kiddle	14	15
R. T. Mark	14	14
H. E. Mealing	14	14
R. C. Phillips	14	15
G. G. Bell	13	16
H. A. Hamersley	13	13
E. C. Hoy	13	13
F. J. Stephen	13	13
H. C. Bath	12	12
J. D. Belgrave	12	17
L. Bennett	12	12
F. J. Davies	12	12

Name	Score in S.E.5	Total Score
E. A. Clear	12	12
R. J. Landis	12	12
R. Manser	12	12
R. I. Marvel	12	12
N. W. R. Mawle	12	12
J. S. Ralston	12	12
A. W. Saunders	12	12
W. A Tyrell	12	17
A. Beck	11	11
P. S. Burge	11	11
W. J. A. Duncan	11	11
H. G. Forrest	11	11
S. B. Horn	11	13
H. R. Kwin	11	11
W. H. Longton	11	11
T. Rose	11	11
E. O. Amos	10	10
F. E. Brown	10	10
S. Carlin	10	10
R. L. Chidlaw-Roberts	10	10
C. W. Cudmore	10	10
E. G. Davies	10	10
T. Durrant	10	11
E. E. Gibbs	10	10
C. D. B. Green	10	11
W. L. Harrison	10	12
W. E. Jenkins	10	10
D. Knight	10	10
G. H. Lewis	10	12
M. C. McGregor	10	11
I. P. R. Napier	10	12
I. L. Roy	10	10
A. Ball	9	44

SOURCES

BOOKS

Bishop, W. A., *Winged Warfare* (Toronto, 1918)

Bowyer, C., *Albert Ball VC* (London, 1977)

Child, S. and C. F. Caunter, *A Historical Summary of the Royal Aircraft Factory and its Antecedents: 1878-1918* (RAE)

Grinnell-Milne, D., *Wind in the Wires* (London, 1933)

Lambert, W. C., *Combat Report* (London, 1973)

Lewis, C., *Sagittarius Rising* (London, 1936)

Lewis, G. H., *Wings over the Somme* (London, 1976)

MacLanachan, W., *Fighter Pilot* (London, 1920)

McCudden, J., *Five Years in the Royal Flying Corps* (London, 1918)

Penrose, H., *British Aviation: The Great War and Armistice* (London, 1969)

Raleigh, W. and H. A. Jones, *The War in the Air* (London, 1922-27)

Sholto-Douglas, W., *Years of Combat* (London, 1963)

Springs, E. W., *War Birds: The Diary of an Unknown Aviator* (New York, 1927)

Sturtevant R. and G. Page, *The S.E.5 File* (Tunbridge Wells, 1996)

MAGAZINES

Flight Magazine – various issues (1915 to date)

The Journal of Cross and Cockade International – various issues

WW1 Aero – various issues

OFFICIAL REPORTS AND PUBLICATIONS

National Archives: various files from the categories: AIR 1, AVIA6, AVIA14, CAB, DSIR, and WO
Report No. AERO 2150 (1947)
RFC Communiqués (1918)
RFC, RAF, and Air Board Rigging Notes and Technical Manuals

PERSONAL DIARIES AND LOGBOOKS

Busk, E. T., Notebooks (photocopy in author's collection)
Folland, H. P., Notebooks 1912-16 (facsimile copies)
Havilland, Geoffrey de, Flight Log 1911-13 (facsimile copy)
O'Gorman, M., Diary (RAE Library)
RFC and RAF pilots' Log Book (RAF Museum)

ACKNOWLEDGEMENTS

In researching the material upon which this book is based, I have received help, either with information or with photographs, from many people, to each of whom due acknowledgement and my grateful thanks should be given. These include: the late Jack Bruce, Mick Davis, Nick Forder, Peter Green, Eric Harlin, Colin and Barbara Huston, Phillip Jarrett, Kevin Kelly, Andy Kemp, Brian Kervell, the late Phillip Kraus, Paul Leaman, Stuart Leslie, Leo Opdycke, Colin Owers, R. B. Pope, Peter Pountney, Jim Prendergast, Mike Speakman, and numerous members of Cross & Cockade International, WW1 aeroplanes Inc., and the Farnborough Air Sciences Trust Association.

Any omissions from this list are due to oversight, not ingratitude, and those few people who promised such help and then failed to deliver are hereby forgiven, for I am sure that their offers were well meant.

I should like to thank my wife Linda for her unfailing patience and support throughout the lengthy process of the preparation of this book, and also to thank my good friend Bob Bellisio, a retired teacher, who proof read key passages of the manuscript, and whose suggestions were always helpful, although any mistakes, of course, remain my own responsibility.

Paul R. Hare
February 2013

INDEX